TEACHING VISUAL LITERACY

USING COMIC BOOKS, GRAPHIC NOVELS, ANIME, CARTOONS, AND MORE TO DEVELOP COMPREHENSION AND THINKING SKILLS

NANCY FREY • DOUGLAS FISHER

EDITORS

CORWIN PRESS
A SAGE Company
Thousand Oaks, CA 91320

For information:

Corwin Press
A SAGE Company
2455 Teller Road
Thousand Oaks,
    California 91320
www.corwinpress.com

SAGE Ltd.
1 Oliver's Yard
55 City Road
London EC1Y 1SP
United Kingdom

SAGE India Pvt. Ltd.
B 1/I 1 Mohan Cooperative
    Industrial Area
Mathura Road, New Delhi 110 044
India

SAGE Asia-Pacific Pte. Ltd.
33 Pekin Street #02-01
Far East Square
Singapore 048763

Printed in the United States of America.

Library of Congress Cataloging-in-Publication Data

Teaching visual literacy : using comic books, graphic novels, anime, cartoons, and more to develop comprehension and thinking skills/editors, Nancy Frey, Douglas Fisher.
       p. cm.
Includes bibliographical references and index.
ISBN 978-1-4129-5311-5 (cloth)
ISBN 978-1-4129-5312-2 (pbk.)
    1. Visual literacy. 2. Visual learning. 3. Reading (Elementary)
4. Cognition in children. I. Frey, Nancy, 1959- II. Fisher, Douglas, 1965-
III. Title.

LB1068.T43 2008
372.6'044—dc22   2007033944

This book is printed on acid-free paper.

08 09 10 11 12 10 9 8 7 6 5 4 3 2 1

Acquisitions Editor:	Cathy Hernandez
Editorial Assistant:	Megan Bedell
Production Editor:	Jenn Reese
Copy Editor:	Paula Bonilla
Typesetter:	C&M Digitals (P) Ltd.
Proofreader:	Andrea Martin
Indexer:	Nara Wood
Cover Designer:	Monique Hahn

Contents

Acknowledgments

Corwin Press gratefully acknowledges the contributions of the following reviewers:

A. Jonathan Eakle
Assistant Professor of Teacher Development and Leadership;
  Reading Program Director
The Johns Hopkins University
Baltimore, MD

Jude Huntz
Sixth Grade English Teacher
The Barstow School
Kansas City, MO

Louanne Clayton Jacobs
Assistant Professor of Reading and Literacy
Alabama A&M University
Madison, AL

Sara Kajder
Assistant Professor of Education
Virginia Tech
Blacksburg, VA

Kathleen Martineau
World History Teacher
South Gate Middle School
South Gate, CA

Alden J. Moe
Professor of Education
Rollins College
Winter Park, FL

Rosemary Palmer
Associate Professor of Literacy Education
Boise State University
Boise, ID

Joy L. Wiggins
Assistant Professor of Curriculum and Instruction
University of Texas, Arlington
Arlington, TX

Lisa Zawilinski
New Literacies Researcher
University of Connecticut
Storrs, CT

About the Editors

Nancy Frey, PhD, is an Associate Professor of Literacy in the School of Teacher Education at San Diego State University. She is a recipient of the Christa McAuliffe award for excellence in teacher education from the American Association of State Colleges and Universities. She has co-authored several books on literacy, and was a co-recipient (with Doug Fisher) of NCTE's 2004 Kate and Paul Farmer award for outstanding writing for their article, "Using Graphic Novels, Anime, and the Internet in an Urban High School," published in *English Journal.* She teaches a variety of courses in elementary and secondary literacy in content area instruction and the support of students with diverse learning needs.

Douglas Fisher, PhD, is a Professor of Language and Literacy Education in the Department of Teacher Education at San Diego State University. He is also the Co-Director for the Center for the Advancement of Reading at the California State University Chancellor's Office. He is the recipient of an International Reading Association Celebrate Literacy Award, the Farmer award for excellence in writing from the National Council of Teachers of English, as well as a Christa McAuliffe award for excellence in teacher education. He has published numerous articles on reading and literacy, differentiated instruction, and curriculum design, as well as books including *Creating Literacy-Rich Schools for Adolescents* (with Gay Ivey), *Improving Adolescent Literacy: Strategies at Work* (with Nancy Frey), and *Teaching English Language Learners: A Differentiated Approach* (with Carol Rothenberg). A former early intervention specialist and language development specialist, he has also taught high school English, writing, and literacy development to public school students.

About the Contributors

Lawrence Baines writes on literacy, technology, and social change. His latest book is *Literacy Through Multisensory Learning*, published by ASCD. He is the editor of www.secondaryenglish.com and posts selected work on his personal Web site at www.lawrencebaines.com.

Lynell Burmark is an Associate in the Thornburg Center for Professional Development, holds two master's degrees and a PhD from Stanford University, and is in frequent demand as a speaker, trainer, writer, strategist, and consultant. Her groundbreaking multimedia workshop "Strategies for Successful Presentations" and her award-winning book *Visual Literacy: Learn to See, See to Learn* (ASCD) quickly established her as a leader in visual literacy and its practical applications for powerful communications. As a K–16 teacher and administrator, Dr. Burmark has been recognized for her many creative accomplishments in multicultural understanding and use of technology in education. Dr. Burmark can be reached at www .lynellburmark.org.

James Bucky Carter is currently a visiting instructor of English/English Education at the University of Southern Mississippi and is completing his PhD in English Education at the University of Virginia. His interests are the pedagogical intersections between sequential art and literacy. His work has been accepted in outlets such as *ImageTexT, English Journal, Contemporary Literary Criticism*, and *International Journal of Comic Art*. He edited and contributed to *Building Literacy Connections With Graphic Novels: Page by Page, Panel by Panel.*

Kelly Chandler-Olcott is an Associate Professor in Syracuse University's Reading and Language Arts Center, where she directs the English Education program. A former secondary English teacher, she conducts research on adolescents' technology-mediated literacy practices, classroom-based inquiry by teachers, and content literacy. Her work has been published in journals such as *English Education, Journal of Adolescent & Adult Literacy*, and *Reading Research Quarterly*. Her most recent books include *Tutoring Adolescent Literacy Learners: A Guide for Volunteers* (2005) with Kathleen Hinchman and *A Land We Can Share: Literacy for Students With Autism* (forthcoming) with Paula Kluth.

Paula Kluth is a consultant, teacher, author, advocate, and independent scholar who works with teachers and families to provide inclusive opportunities for students with disabilities. She earned her PhD in Special Education at the University of Wisconsin. Her research and professional interests include differentiating instruction, and supporting students with autism and significant disabilities in inclusive classrooms. She is the author of *"You're Going to Love This Kid": Educating Students With Autism in Inclusive Classrooms* and the lead editor of *Access to Academics: Critical Approaches to Inclusive Curriculum, Instruction, and Policy.*

Jacquelyn McTaggart taught lower elementary school children in Minnesota and Iowa public schools for more than four decades. The author of *From the Teacher's Desk* and a frequent speaker at International Reading Association conferences, Jacquie also operates an interactive teacher-to-parent Web site at www.theteachersdesk.com, writes a weekly news column on education issues and parenting practices that affect the learning process, writes for a variety of teaching publications and academic journals, and teaches creative writing classes at two Iowa community colleges.

Lawrence R. Sipe is an Associate Professor in the Graduate School of Education at the University of Pennsylvania, where he is a member of the Reading/Writing/Literacy Program. He teaches courses in children's and adolescent literature, including picturebooks through Young Adult Fiction. His research interests focus on the ways in which young children indicate literary understanding and visual aesthetic awareness during readalouds of picture storybooks. His PhD is in children's literature and early literacy from The Ohio State University, and his master's degree is in Psychology of Reading and Special Education from Temple University.

Rocco Versaci is a Professor of English at Palomar College, located in San Marcos, California. He teaches various composition, creative writing, and literature courses, including a class on comic books. In addition, he serves as co-advisor of Palomar's literary magazine, *Bravura*. He earned his PhD in English from Indiana University in 1997, and since then he has authored several pieces on comics, including *This Book Contains Graphic Language: Comics as Literature.* Dr. Versaci lives in North San Diego County with his wife and two sons.

Thomas D. Wolsey is an educational consultant and adjunct professor of literacy education. He taught English and United States History at the middle school level. Presently he is completing a doctoral program at San Diego State University/University of San Diego. His interests are in writing pedagogy and the intersections of literacy and technology.

Introduction

Nancy Frey and Douglas Fisher

Seeing comes before words. The child looks and recognizes before it can speak. (Berger, 2006, p. 681)

Berger speaks of the way human language evolves—first sight and recognition, then speaking, later reading and writing. Yet he also evokes a truth that is lost in the trample of teaching the formal literacies— that visual images play an integral part in understanding. The elements of literacy are commonly described as *reading, writing, speaking,* and *listening. Viewing* is mentioned in passing, if at all. When visuals *are* utilized, it is often in service of the other literacies. We speak of visualizing as a reading comprehension strategy, or discuss the importance of crafting strong images in writing. But notice how we indicate understanding in everyday speech: "I see what you mean."

We think of visual literacy as describing the complex act of meaning making using still or moving images. As with reading comprehension, visually literate learners are able to make connections, determine importance, synthesize information, evaluate, and critique. Further, these visual literacies are interwoven with textual ones, so that their interaction forms the basis for a more complete understanding. The twenty-first-century learner must master this intermediality of images and text in order to interpret an increasingly digital world (Lapp, Flood, & Fisher, 1999).

Ultimately, a fundamental goal of education is to teach effective communication. It is the message that lies at the heart of communication, be it verbal, written, or pictorial, and the challenge to any communicator is to create accurate messages and interpret the messages of others with equal skill. Hobbs (1997) describes a set of assumptions about the key analytic concepts of literacy in the age of information:

- All messages are constructions.
- Messages are representations of social reality.

- Individuals negotiate meaning by interacting with messages.
- Messages have economic, political, social, and aesthetic purposes.
- Each form of communication has unique characteristics. (p. 9)

Whether they are discussing a novel in a literature circle, listening to a peer describe a visit to the zoo, reading a math textbook, or writing a science lab report, their success is dependent on their ability to master the message. As well, in each case there is likely to be a visual element. The novel may have illustrations, the peer may bring a video of the trip, the math textbook may contain a diagram, the science lab report may include sketches of what was observed. Yet these elements of the message are unlikely to be addressed in any formal way.

Hobbs' key analytical concepts also describe the critical literacy stance necessary for interpretation of print and visual messages. The emphasis of critical literacy is less about acquisition of skills and more about questioning the author's purpose, searching for alternative meanings, and considering the role identity plays. A critical literacy lens assumes that all text is constructed from a particular viewpoint, and that the reader or viewer must analyze the message for who or what is left out. This may include discussions on power, marginalization, and perspective. Again, visual literacy assumes an important position. How does a fictionalized account of a historical event influence understanding? Films like *Amadeus* and *Amistad* have been criticized for playing loose with the facts. How do illustrations influence the meaning of the text? The picture book *Nappy Hair* (Herron, 1998) was at the center of a controversy in New York City because photocopied illustrations from the book were viewed by some as demeaning to African American children. Do comic books and graphic novels constitute an appropriate genre for classroom instruction? School boards, curriculum directors, parents, and teachers all over the country view these materials in very different ways. It would seem that critical literacy, as it applies to visual literacy, is a stance that educators must assume on behalf of their learners.

This book was conceived as a means for examining visual literacy in just that fashion. We invited authors and researchers from around the country to describe their view of an aspect of visual literacy. We gave them a tall order—provide background information on the subject, describe ways in which they use visual literacy tools in their instructional practices, and give the reader some ideas for how to apply it to his or her own classroom.

In Chapter 1, Lynell Burmark introduces visual literacy as a tool for learning. She discusses principles, such as the effect of color, and advises teachers on how to use visual images in the classroom. She fills her own work with images to illustrate these elements—truly a case of a picture being worth a thousand words.

In Chapter 2, Jacquelyn McTaggart, a teacher with 42 years of experience, provides an overview of graphic novels, perhaps the fastest-growing literary form in publishing today. Students seem to know about this—we've all seen them squirreled away in backpacks. Yet relatively few teachers use graphic novels regularly in their classrooms. This may be in part because they are unfamiliar. This chapter will rapidly build your comfort and confidence with this form of visual narrative.

After this overview of graphic novels, James Bucky Carter challenges the status quo of text selection in the classroom in Chapter 3. A growing body of knowledge suggests that visual literacy is essential in the twenty-first century, yet resistance to the form persists, especially at the secondary level. Carter's provocative chapter may not elicit universal agreement, but it is certain to get the conversation started about policy and practice in what students read and don't read in our classrooms.

In Chapter 4, Kelly Chandler-Olcott extends the conversation about visual literacy with a review of anime, an animation art form originated in Japan, and manga, its print-based form. Millions of young people view and create anime, yet they are rarely seen inside classrooms. Chandler-Olcott provides a history of these forms and explains that a view of multiple literacies requires inclusion of the visual language of anime. She also describes the perspectives of consumers of anime and manga and provides examples of how they can be used in K–12 classrooms.

Rocco Versaci takes a close look at comic books in Chapter 5, beginning with their history and the role of censorship in the 1950s in undermining the integrity of this genre. The author goes on to describe the visual and literary elements to be found in high quality comics and provides readers with three of his own lessons on the use of comics to teach visual literacy.

Moving from comics to political cartoons, in Chapter 6 Thomas DeVere Wolsey analyzes this form using the perspectives central to visual literacy. Long valued by history teachers for educating learners about the political, social, and cultural climate, the author further expands political cartoons by drawing on experiential learning theory and iconography. In addition, he describes a framework called Cartoon Thinking for understanding this form.

In Chapter 7, Lawrence R. Sipe deepens our understanding of visual literacy through a close look at picturebooks. Although we are surrounded from birth by them, this literary form is rarely understood for its visual sophistication. Sipe presents a scholarly analysis of the aesthetics of picturebooks, as well as examples of the language of young children as they utilize visual literacy to make meaning.

Lawrence Baines discusses film as visual literacy in Chapter 8. The author offers examples of student work in vocabulary, grammar, and writing as it relates to moving images. This is not a version of a film appreciation class—Baines is interested in using the medium to broaden students' understanding of the language of film, and to turn it into a form of expression and creativity. Seen through the lens of film, literacy through reading, writing, and speaking takes a fresh approach.

In Chapter 9, Paula Kluth rounds out the book by describing the ways in which visual literacy tools can be used to extend the understanding of students with disabilities, and to provide them with another means of expressing what they know and think about a subject. The examples of student work included in the chapter broaden our understanding of the power of visual literacy.

You may be new to visual literacy as a classroom practice, or expert in the subject. In either case, we hope that the ideas described in this book provoke discussion and ideas. We are reminded of an item in Robert Fulghum's *All I Really Need to Know I Learned in Kindergarten:* "Remember the Dick-and-Jane books and the first word you learned—the biggest word of all—LOOK" (p. 3). We invite you to do the same.

REFERENCES

Berger, J. (2006). Ways of seeing. In D. McQuade & C. McQuade (Eds.), *Seeing and writing 3* (pp. 681–693). Boston: Bedford/St. Martin's.

Fulghum, R. (2003). *All I really need to know I learned in kindergarten.* New York: Ballantine.

Herron, C. (1998). *Nappy hair.* New York: Dragonfly.

Hobbs, R. (1997). Literacy for the information age. In J. Flood, S. B. Heath, & D. Lapp (Eds.), *Research on teaching literacy through the communicative and visual arts* (pp. 7–14). New York: Macmillan.

Lapp, D., Flood, J., & Fisher, D. (1999). Intermediality: How the use of multiple media enhances learning. *The Reading Teacher, 52*(7), 776–780.

1

Visual Literacy

What You Get Is What You See

Lynell Burmark

What exactly is meant by the term "visual literacy"? In what ways does it play a role in learning? Burmark introduces the term and explains how images influence understanding.

In the 1998 film *The Horse Whisperer,* a woman spends most of a day trying to find a horse ranch hidden somewhere in the bewildering splendor of Montana. When she finally arrives, she apologizes for being late, explaining, "There weren't any signs."

"There were lots of signs," the film's title character replies. "Just none that you could read."

Indeed, signs are everywhere—for those who can read them. Because of television, advertising, and the Internet, the primary literacy of the twenty-first century is visual. It's no longer enough to read and write text. Our students must learn to process both words *and* pictures. To be visually literate, they must learn to "read" (consume/interpret) images and "write" (produce/use) visually rich communications. They must be able to move gracefully and fluently between text and images, between literal and figurative worlds.

OUR VISUAL WORLD

No one would disagree that we live in a visual world. From the billboards lining our freeways to the steady flow of video feeds clamoring for our attention, we can't escape the visual influx. Even text has taken on a visual aspect.

In the *TV Guide* advertisement found in Figure 1.1 for an "extreme makeover," notice the dressmaker's dummy standing in for the letter *i*. Consider the energy exuded by the Entertainment Network logo. That exclamation point, which is bright red in the original advertisement, has probably convinced us that this will be exciting television even before we switch on the program. After all, according to the old adage, seeing is believing.

Figure 1.1

We are discovering that seeing is also remembering. The McCormick Tribune Freedom Museum reported the following results from a poll testing our knowledge of First Amendment rights:

- 22 percent of U.S. citizens surveyed could name all five family members in *The Simpsons* television cartoon.
- However, only 1 in 1,000 (0.1 percent) could name all five freedoms guaranteed under the First Amendment of the Bill of Rights.
- 20 percent thought the right to own a pet was protected and the right to drive was guaranteed, although the car was not invented for another 100 years. ("Homer Simpson, Yes," 2006)

Youth are definitely accustomed to getting their content from visual media. A study by Yale University reported that the average U.S. elementary school student watched between five and six hours of television a day.

By the time students graduated from high school, they had logged some 22,000 hours of television (Dunn, 1994).

Figure 1.2

Printed with permission.

BRAIN BANDWIDTH

Part of the reason that images are so powerful is due in part to the way we are wired, physiologically. Robert Lindstrom (1999) has emphasized the importance of sight in perception and communication. Lindstrom, author of *The Business Week Guide to Multimedia Presentations*, explains:

> Of all our sense receptors, the eyes are the most powerful information conduit to the brain. They send information to the cerebral cortex through two optic nerves, each consisting of 1,000,000 nerve fibers. By comparison, each auditory nerve consists of a mere 30,000 fibers.
> Nerve cells devoted to visual processing . . . account for about 30% of the brain's cortex, compared to 8% for touch and 3% for hearing. With all the bandwidth to the brain, it's no wonder we perceive the world and communicate in visual terms. We register a full-color image, the equivalent of a megabyte of data, in a fraction of a second.

Research from 3M Corporation indicates that humans process visuals an astounding 60,000 times faster than text ("Polishing Your Presentation,"

2001). For educators pressured to cover inordinate amounts of material before the test *du jour,* using visuals is a way to speed things up 60,000 times! Using visuals might even provide time for music, art, drama, social interaction, and project-based learning!

Should you question the speed of visual processing, consider the task of describing a classroom full of students. To do so in words would take an eternity. The adorable freckled face of the redhead in the second row might take a whole paragraph in itself. And what about the clothing, hair, and facial expression of each student? It would be a daunting task. Alternatively, pick up a camera with a wide-angle lens, and, with one click, an image of the entire class has been captured. Words by their very nature are *sequential,* like a string of letters typed on a keyboard. Images, on the other hand, are *simultaneous* – everyone becomes part of the picture at the same time.

We know how certain photographs can convey a wealth of information. Take, for example, Figure 1.3, a snapshot of a grandfather with his first granddaughter.

I have shown this image in many different countries. Whatever their cultural backgrounds, people invariably recognize the relationship and, invariably, they feel the love. When viewing an image, the eyes have certain proclivities. Take a look at Figure 1.4, a yin-yang diagram from Adobe Systems.

Where does your eye go? Most people will be drawn to the right side of the diagram because the eye goes to pictures before words or numbers.

Figure 1.3

Figure 1.4

Do advertisers understand this phenomenon? Examine any of the myriad of pharmaceutical product advertisements flooding the market today. You will usually see a large, full-color, photographic image of healthy, satisfied, attractive, happy people. Then search for the list of potential side effects. These will be printed in tiny black type on a boring white background.

As a way of teaching students about the power of visuals in advertising, I suggest having students bring in copies of a range of such pharmaceutical advertisements. Pick the best of the collection and then assign groups of six students to select an advertisement and redo it, illustrating the side effects in color and listing the potential benefits in tiny type on a white background with the caveat: "Results may vary." When students display the original advertisements next to their created alternatives, a lively discussion will erupt focused on why the advertising agencies chose to illustrate certain aspects of their product and not others.

A FEW COMPELLING REASONS

Why use images in classroom instruction? Obviously, we can use images and video to break down the walls of the classroom and take our students places they have never been before. It's a lot more fun to *see* the sign for Nobody's Inn outside Anchorage, Alaska, than to merely *hear* about it (Figure 1.5).

What about engagement? We've all observed that computer games and visually rich educational software can draw students like magnets (Figure 1.6).

Figure 1.5

Figure 1.6

Probably the most compelling reason for using images in instruction is that images are stored in long-term memory. Unlike factoids and phone numbers that can "go in one ear and out the other," images are indelibly etched in our long-term memory. We are more apt to remember a person's face than that person's name. The implications for achievement testing are obvious. The key is to make sure students have a picture in their "mind's eye" of the important concepts and content that they will need to recall.

WORDS VERSUS IMAGES

Here's another activity to try with your students. Ask everyone in the room to draw a cat. Ask whether they all drew pointy ears, whiskers, perhaps a long tail. Ask whether they feel that the person next to them would recognize their drawing as a cat.

Next ask students to draw a civet cat. Assuming no one in your class has ever seen one, you'll get cries of "What?" and similar utterances of frustration. You can easily find an image of a civet cat on the Internet. (They are members of the *Viverridae* family and more closely resemble the mongoose than they do the domestic felines we keep as household pets.) Point out to the class that it's almost impossible to draw with accuracy something they have never seen, then reassure them: "It's OK to ask for more information when I mention anything that you haven't seen before."

What's the bottom line? Words are used to *recall* things we have already seen and experienced. This is why writing is so much more detailed and evocative when students can look at an image before they start writing. A wonderful Title IVC project called "Images in the Writing Process" asked first graders to create collages with colorful pieces of tissue paper.

The student who made the collage shown in Figure 1.7 went on to write a story in which she described clouds "like fluffy pink pancakes." Would she ever have "seen" those clouds in such a vivid way without having first created the collage?

When students are first learning to read, particularly if they have had limited life and language experience, comic strips and comic books can be a fun way to make the image-word association. The visual clues make it more probable that the students will have a positive experience while reading and feel encouraged to read more. The Internet can be an excellent resource for comics, such as the official Peanuts Web site, www.snoopy.com.

In "Teaching Visual Literacy in a Multimedia Age," Glenda Rakes (1999) claimed that, by combining visuals and text, we can increase comprehension:

Using positron emission tomography (PET scans), medical researchers have been able to demonstrate that different areas of

Figure 1.7

Used with permission.

the brain become active when individuals are exposed to verbal and visual information. When individuals were asked to look at and remember verbal information, two regions in the brain's verbal domain—the left hemisphere—became active. When presented with visual information, the right hemisphere lit up.

Given this information, the use of visuals in instructional materials takes on a larger dimension than when simply thought of as decorative supplements to text. The use of visuals with text can provide that dual code that can, in turn, increase comprehension. (pp. 14–15)

Award-winning teacher Jerome Burg has put this theory into practice in his high school English classroom. He assigns groups of students to read classic works of literature and then demonstrate their understanding by creating short comic-book versions of the works. Can you guess what play Figure 1.8 depicts?

Recently Burg applied this concept to ComicLife, a computer program that allows students to create comic books using digital photographs (Figure 1.9). When his students are required to "choreograph" a scene and to "stage" a series of photographs, they end up identifying more closely with the characters, exploring them from "within the roles" rather than as silent observers.

Figure 1.8

Figure 1.9

Once students can empathize with the characters, in this case Romeo and Juliet, they can address essential questions associated with character development, motivations behind the protagonists and antagonists, the tragic or comic consequences of their actions, and basic themes in the story. As Burg explained to me:

> It's absolutely amazing to me to watch students process the primary elements of a story, setting, character, plot and theme, from the vantage point of a producer of images. One limitation of comic books is that they are restricted to only a very few "cells" and to very abbreviated dialogue. This forces students to synthesize the elements of the story down to the essence. If they have studied symbolism and foreshadowing and other literary techniques, students must figure out how to capture these complex ideas in spite of the fact that characters can only speak 8–10 words at a time and they can only use 6–10 visual cells to tell the story. The discussions over "what has to go in" and "what isn't necessary" have the students contemplating at very deep levels and they often get pretty "animated" themselves!

COLOR POWER

A big part of the impact of images is the color. We can look at a color image of a natural landscape, for example, and immediately identify the season as autumn—even before we notice the fallen leaves.

Figure 1.10

Used with permission from Lou Fournier Marzeles.

Recent research concerning the benefits of using color in presentations indicated:

- Color visuals increase willingness to read by up to 80 percent
- Using color can increase motivation and participation by up to 80 percent
- Color enhances learning and improves retention by more than 75 percent. ("The Power of Color," 2007)

Approximately 80 percent of our impression of a product is based on its color (*"Brand Packaging Magazine,"* 2000). Advertisers understand this and use color in packaging so they appear to meet our needs. Advertisers know that our autonomic response to the colors, rather than the aesthetics of the packaging, determines what we buy (Wagner, 1985).

What are the implications of this for educators? Traditionally, we think of color as the decorative element for our bulletin boards: orange for Halloween, Thanksgiving, and autumn; pastels for Easter and spring; and so on. But color is much more than decoration. We are biologically programmed to respond to the colors we see:

Red   Danger, excitement

Blue   Calm, security

Pink   Tranquility, relaxation

Green Fertility, creativity

Specific colors often evoke predictable responses:

- Yellow is the most attention grabbing of all the 16.7 million colors the human eye can see. (Think of yellow highlighters. Why do they work so well?)
- Black signals authority and finality. (Think of judges' robes and "fade to black" screens for scene changes in movies. Consider judicious use of black in your own slideshow presentations.)

Researchers have documented the impact of color on comprehension and recall (Hoadley, Simmons, & Gilroy, 2000). How might this knowledge be applied to preparing documents for classroom use?

Figure 1.11

Activity	Improved Up To
Time to sort documents	15%
Time to locate a **target word** within a document	74%
Accuracy of comprehension	77%

What are the "target words" in your documents? Due dates? Key pieces of information? What color might you choose for those target words? Did you answer "Red"? Wagner (1985) has explored the reasons behind the power of red:

> Particularly yellow-based reds (tomato) are great attention-getters. They have the power to get noticed, quickly. There was an early belief that red (rather than yellow) was really the fastest color seen, and this early myth was the basis for red being used for fire engines and other emergency equipment. Red used in combination with yellow will get even more attention than either color alone. (p. 37)

Other colors, like the sepia tone used in the original of this photograph, alert us to the vintage era of a picture.

Figure 1.12

PETERSON STUDIO—TACOMA

For baby boomers and older folk, sepia evokes nostalgia for times gone by. (This photo is particularly evocative for me, as it's my parents' wedding photo from 1938.)

Colors can also trigger a *physiological* response. Fire-engine red in particular makes the blood race as it grabs attention and promises excitement, passion, and potential danger. It's not surprising that on any given day nineteen of the twenty cars displayed at my local Corvette dealership are red.

Another color, yellow, draws attention even faster than red. Think high-lighter pens, taxis, warning signs, and daffodils. As graphic artists say, "Yellow pops." That is why yellow is the best color for text in PowerPoint slides.

The color blue, by contrast, recedes into the background—like the sky beyond the horizon, like the far-stretching surface of the lake, like the ocean's glistening waves. Blue serves as a calming backdrop for popping yellow letters.

Green is associated with creativity and new birth, trees and leaves, and even with healthy food. Have your students check out the latest packaging for Crisco shortening. With its color background and clever choice of words, if you didn't know better, you'd think that Crisco was a fat-free health food!

FROM THE ABSTRACT TO THE CONCRETE

If you say the word "rose," and then ask your students to "make an image" in their mind's eye, how many will see exactly this rose?

Why or why not? Which is more tangible, more concrete—the image or the words? If you want all the students to be "on the same page," seeing the same flower at the same time, what is the fastest, most certain way to get them there (short of actually handing them the real rose)?

Figure 1.13

DO YOU SEE WHAT I SEE?

As "concrete" as images are, they still leave room for interpretation. I tested out this theory by donning hot pink hair and big turquoise sunglasses (Figure 1.14).

It's the real me. Knowing that we are all quick to judge from appearances, I considered delivering a keynote presentation dressed like this to see how seriously the audience would take me and my message.

Although friends and colleagues have dared—OK, double-dared—me to make a pink-haired entrance for real, I haven't had the nerve to do so . . . as yet. Instead, I sent a color slide to teacher friends at the middle school and high school levels to get students' reactions to the image. Without identifying me, my friends asked their students to write down what they thought of the pink lady: age, occupation, character, thoughts, and so on.

- Trevor, a middle-schooler, wrote: This lady is 45 years old. She is an undercover FBI agent. She is a nice person but could be different in her disguises. She is probably thinking about how she can see who is going to steal the Mona Lisa painting.

Figure 1.14

Used with permission from Lou Fournier Marzeles.

- Liz, a high-schooler, wrote: This woman grew up in middle to upper class society because she has straight teeth, meaning when she was younger she had braces. Her real age is of no importance. She is young at heart; you can tell by the smile. Material possessions aren't of any value because she isn't wearing any jewelry. That and she probably spends a lot of time around children who like to pull on necklaces and earrings. You can see a few strands of her own light brown hair that she doesn't feel she needs to dye, despite incoming gray hairs. She is comfortable with who she is.

What were the students doing in these cases? How much of their judgment came from associating my photo with images of comparable people in their lives or whom they had seen in movies or on television? Particularly in Liz's case, how much did her life experience and her own "issues" color her evaluation? Do you think she had braces? Wanted braces? Had a mother who wore expensive jewelry? Dyed her hair? In the words of Anaïs Nin, "We don't see things as they are; we see them as we are."

THE POWER OF FIRST IMPRESSIONS

We spend our lives filling the hard drive of our minds with images, and we do our best to file new information where it best connects to or associates with data that is already there. Pink hair? More likely to be a nightclub singer than a college professor. Five nose rings and several visible tattoos? More likely to be a biker than an Episcopal priest. Is this prejudice? Or is it just the mind trying to make sense of a universe bombarding it with images?

And it isn't just *people* we judge by first impressions. The strongest and most indelible impressions of *places* come from their initial, visual impact. Spear (1995) writes:

> First impressions account for more than 50% of the entire experience of a place. We create impressions in the early stages of experiencing an environment, and they remain a nearly indelible part of it even as changes occur and we process new information. (p. 61)

POWERPOINT TIPS

According to Tad Simons, editor-in-chief of *Presentations* magazine, some 30 million PowerPoint presentations are given around the world every day. Most of them use the standard templates and fill every screen with bulleted text. Besides the fact that such presentations are innately boring, the research now tells us that retention and transfer of learning both go down when the presenter reads text from the slides (Mayer, 1995). In my live presentations, I often ask audience members to vote on which of the following three slides is the most effective:

1. All text

2. Text with a small image

3. Full screen, color photographic image

The answer, of course, is number three, but—OK, it was a trick question—with voiceover narration. Show the image, then narrate the information that you want to anchor to that image. That way both the visual and auditory modes are doing what they do best. Yes, visual and verbal information are encoded and decoded by separate, specialized perceptual and cognitive channels in the brain. (This is what Paivio calls "dual coding.") But, as Paivio (1986) noted, the brain coordinates these independent systems so that concepts can flow seamlessly between their linguistic labels and their visual representations.

Mayer (2001) shares his research findings that anchor images with voiceover narration increase recall and retention (regurgitating information for the test) by an average of 42 percent. And what's even more exciting for educators is that transfer (actual long-term learning and application of that learning) is boosted a whopping 89 percent.

BEGIN WITH AN ANCHOR IMAGE

It's time for teachers to arm themselves with Mayer's research and to take advantage of the way kids entertain themselves today, to employ those same media (video, images with voiceovers) and the thinking habits they foster for the betterment of student learning. Every classroom should have an LCD projector. When the students enter the classroom, a compelling image should fill the screen. Their job is to sit quietly, for two to three minutes, contemplating what that image means to them. Then, when asked to do so by the teacher, they share their prior knowledge and experience with two or three other students sitting around them. After that, a whole class discussion ensues. The teacher may ask leading questions to extract more information and ideas from the students. In some instances, the teacher may post the image (on his or her Web site) and ask the students to ferret out additional information as homework. An excellent example, should you be teaching U.S. history or women's studies, is Figure 1.15.

Typing the words "We can do it!" into the Google search engine will bring up this image and the story behind it. But the key is not to find the right answer, but to "unpack" the image for all its implications. By "unpacking," a term coined by my colleague Lou Fournier Marzeles, we mean the

Figure 1.15

ability to discern the underlying, intended significance (witting or unwitting) of any image. Unpacking does not require advanced education in psychology or a preternatural gift for intuiting the hidden meanings of pictures.

Unpacking is a far more prosaic and accessible skill that simply requires the ability to ask certain questions about any picture. These questions might include: *Why did the creator of this image—the photographer, cinematographer, painter, computer artist, and so on—choose to make this particular image in the first place?*

While often a seemingly obvious question, it serves us well to ask it anyway; it helps begin the process of discernment. Sometimes the answer is surprising and leads to other helpful inquiries. For example, why did Van Gogh choose to paint sunflowers? Some immediate and apparently obvious answers might be, because he found them beautiful or otherwise intriguing; because their colors lent themselves to vivid expression on canvas; because they looked good in certain rooms. But a deeper speculation might lead one to consider deeper levels of significance behind these answers. *Why* did he find sunflowers beautiful? *Why* might he have considered their colors particularly vivid on canvas? Unpacking images leads to more thoughtful consideration of the all-too-easy obvious, which inherently helps one ponder the creativity (or lack of it) behind imagery at more meaningful, more fulfilling levels.

Why did the image creator choose the particular framing of this image? By framing we mean the exact way in which the content of the image is rendered; this can mean camera angle and composition, coloration, perspective, emphasis of certain features over others, and many other factors.

What is the mood of the image? Is it dark or light in its emotional character? Is it serious or indifferent, beauteous or repellent, jovial or troubling? Why does the image seem to have the emotional quality it does? How much of that comes from the image creator, and how much might be a subjective reaction of the viewer? What makes the difference?

Does the image reflect common societal mores, or does it reflect a uniquely personal value system? What determines the nature of these conditions and values? Is there an overt or inadvertent agenda at work in the image? These are hardly superfluous considerations when it comes to images, for, as we shall see, images inherently and inevitably deliver a powerful impact to the brain and how it processes information.

How does the image make you feel? And why? Contemplation of this invites a fuller understanding of the powerfully affective nature of imagery. To ignore this nature is to leave oneself aimlessly adrift amid countless possible outcomes of the use, and misuse, of images.

RESOURCES FOR IMAGES

The main—and highly recommended—sources for images are student drawings, images taken by teachers and students with digital and cell phone cameras, images from Web sites, and video clips either streamed from the Internet or residing on local servers like Safari Montage.

We all know there are countless resources on the Internet, and we also know that finding the right ones for classroom use can be like plucking raindrops from waves in the ocean. And often, when we do find a great site, just when we think we've captured it, it washes back out to cyber sea never to be found again.

In the thousands of hours I've spent doing research for my publications, presentations, and Web seminars, I have uncovered awesome Web sites with ideas, materials, and breathtaking images. As an aid to teachers, I've listed the best of what I've discovered, with hyperlinks to the sites themselves, in a handout called "Web Resources for Images." I invite you to explore those sites and start using more images in your classroom. You can start by visiting www.educatebetter.org. Go to the Handouts section and type in:

a.   Username: educate

b.   Password: better

WYGIWYS

When my colleague Lou Fournier Marzeles was reviewing my *Visual Literacy* book (Burmark, 2006) with his amazing ability to condense 100 pages into one sentence, he said: "So, what you're talking about is WYGIWYS?"

"*Wiggywhiz?*" I inquired, cluelessly.

"Yes," chimed Lou. "What You *Get* Is What You See. WYGIWYS. You can't understand or 'get' anything until you have a mental image to hook it on."

Getting more and more excited, I replied: "This has serious implications for education. If teachers want all their students 'on the same page,' they really have to introduce their lessons—especially new concepts—with *images* before bombarding the students with *words*."

"Precisely," opined the big picture synthesizer. "Remember you wrote a book to help teachers do just that!"

CENTER STAGE

So, why not teach visual literacy as a means of preparing students for a life in which one of the primary vehicles for communication, the Internet, is based on a graphical interface and where the value of a business is reflected in the success of its visual representation? Why not take a more visual approach to education, and encourage students to illustrate, demonstrate, and celebrate what they learn in their own creative ways, rather than regurgitating irrelevant, decontextualized facts on impersonal, institutionalized, standardized tests?

It's time not only for students to read or consume images, but also to write or produce them in ways that let the students' values, feelings, and achievements take center stage. Follow the example of art teacher Jennifer Gosnell in Covington, Washington, whose students at Tahoma Senior High School make collages of images into logos that represent who they are (Figure 1.16).

Take every opportunity to have students communicate visually. For example, after years of struggling in the library to keep student voices down, Bellevue, Washington, media specialist Judy Bordeaux had students illustrate their "12-inch voices" (Figure 1.17).

With that image indelibly etched in their minds, the rule should have a better chance of sticking!

Traditional instructional practices cannot compete with the likes of MTV. But educators have the advantage—and the opportunity—to involve students in the creation and presentation of their own knowledge. By teaching students to "go visual," to use multimedia to express themselves, we can make our students stars, and our classrooms *center stage* for learning. Sit back and relax. The show is about to begin.

Figure 1.16

Used with permission.

Figure 1.17

Used with permission.

REFERENCES

Brand Packaging magazine noted recently that 80 percent of a consumer's buying decision is based on color. (2000). *Kinko's Impress, 1*(1), 15.

Burmark, L. (2002). *Visual literacy.* Alexandria, VA: Association for Supervision and Curriculum Development.

Burmark, L. (2006). *Visual literacy* (eBook). www.schoolvideos.com

Dunn, J. L. (1994). Television watchers. *Instructor, 103*(8), 50–54.

Hoadley, E. D., Simmons, L. P., & Gilroy, F. D. (2000). Investigating the effects of color, font, and bold highlighting in text for the end user. *Journal of Business and Economic Perspectives, 26*(2), 44–64.

Homer Simpson, yes; First Amendment? "Doh!" (2006, March 1). *Editor & Publisher.* Retrieved March 7, 2007, from http://www.editorandpublisher.com/eandp/news/article_display.jsp?vnu_content_id=1002113807

Lindstrom, R. L. (1999, April 19). Being visual: The emerging visual enterprise. *Business Week* Special Advertising Section.

Mayer, R. E. (2001). *Multimedia learning.* New York: Cambridge University Press.

Paivio, A. (1986). *Mental representations: A dual coding approach.* New York: Oxford University Press.

Polishing your presentation. (2001). *3M meeting network articles and advice.* Retrieved March 7, 2007, from http://www.3m.com/meetingnetwork/readingroom/meetingguide_pres.html

The power of color in presentations. (2001). *3M meeting network articles and advice.* Retrieved March 7, 2007 from: http://www.3m.com/meetingnetwork/readingroom/meetingguide_power_color.html

Rakes, G. C. (1999). Teaching visual literacy in a multimedia age. *Tech Trends, 43*(4), 14–18.

Spear, W. (1995). *Feng shui made easy: Designing your life with the ancient art of placement.* San Francisco: HarperCollins.

Wagner, C. (1985). *Color power.* Chicago: Wagner Institute for Color Research.

2

Graphic Novels

The Good, the Bad, and the Ugly

Jacquelyn McTaggart

Do you know what your students are reading? Graphic novels are increasingly the recreational reading material of choice among children and adolescents, even by those who are not traditionally identified as voluntary readers. This literary form differs from traditional prose text, yet offers excellent potential for classroom use. McTaggart brings us up to speed on these visual texts and explains that using graphic novels only with struggling readers represents a missed opportunity for all students.

In 2001 I began speaking to teachers throughout the country at International Reading Association state and regional conferences. My most requested topic is "Transforming the Reluctant Reader." All went well, and I was quite proud of myself—until one beautiful fall day in 2003.

It happened in Philadelphia where I was speaking to about a thousand reading teachers. I was in the process of wrapping things up and, as usual, asked if anyone had any questions. Quicker than you can say "dummy," a fellow seated in the far back corner stood up and yelled, "How do you feel about the graphic novels so many teachers are using now?"

Uh, oh. Time to 'fess up. "Sir, I'm ashamed to admit that I do not know enough about graphic novels to offer an opinion. Would you allow me to buy you a soda after this session so that you can fill me in?" The audience laughed, I answered a couple of "easy" questions, slunk off the stage, bought two cokes, and began learning about graphic novels.

Many of you undoubtedly know more about graphic novels than I did when I had my "God, please strike me dead—*now*" experience, but perhaps you're still a bit foggy on a few areas. If so, read on. You may find the question that's been lurking in your mind is answered by the information that several experts (colleagues in the trenches) were kind enough to share.

What Is a Graphic Novel?

There are two kinds. The most prevalent (roughly 90 percent) graphic novel is the trade paperback collection of stories initially published serially as comic books. This type normally contains six to twelve comics bound together as one book. The remaining 10 percent is a stand-alone story presented in comics form, but published as a book.

New nonfiction graphic novels are being released regularly and the subject matter varies greatly. The majority of new releases are fantasy. Reluctant and struggling readers prefer the fantasy novels, although most will tolerate the nonfiction—with a little grumbling.

Most graphic novels are soft covered, contain between 130 and 150 pages, and retail for around $10. Schools are usually granted a 20 percent discount and are not taxed. A few graphic novels have hard covers, contain more pages, and can run as high as $35.

Japanese published comics and graphic novels are highly popular with kids throughout the world. Many of these are printed on coarse paper and contain no colored graphics. The ones published in the United States are usually printed in color on glossy white paper. Due to these differences, U.S. published comics are often shorter and more expensive than Japanese ones.

Today the Term "Graphic Novel" Is a Common Buzzword Among Teachers, Librarians, Writers, Artists, and Publicists. What Accounts for This?

In 1991 Art Spiegelman's comic-book-format, soft-covered book *Maus* (the story of his father's experience in the Holocaust) was released, and the term "graphic novel" was coined. *Maus* was awarded the Pulitzer Prize in 1992, and since then the graphic novel's rise has been "faster than a speeding bullet" (Weiner, 2003).

Graphic novels first appeared on *USA Today*'s best-selling books list in 2002. As of this writing, seven titles are on the list, including two from the crime-novel-inspired *Sin City* series by Frank Miller (not recommended for schools). In 2005 Scholastic Books jumped into the graphic-novel pool. Jeff Smith, who self-published his popular *Bone* series in black and white for more than a decade, now colors the frames for a glossy, nine-volume version of Scholastic's new imprint, Graphix.

The bookshelf space given to graphic novels by chain and independent bookstores has raised the medium's profile, and endorsements by respected American publications such as the *New York Times Book Review, Library Journal,* and *Publishers Weekly* are raising the cartooning field's status. In France, one out of every five books sold is a graphic novel. Whether or not that same phenomenon will develop in the United States remains to be seen.

The popularity of the graphic novel (value to be discussed later) is attributable to kids' familiarity with the oft-featured superheroes, their passion for fantasy, action-packed story lines, visual appeal, and the attention graphic novels give to pop culture—what's hot and what's not.

Unless you hide in the custodian's closet all day, you've heard your students talk about *Hulk, Spider-Man, X-Men, Teen Titans,* and other super-heroes. All of these fantasy characters were "born" as comic-book or graphic-novel characters and their sagas were later adapted into TV shows and movies. The apparel industry adopted the characters, and they are now modern-day icons. Some adults scoff at these far-out characters, but kids can't get enough of them. Youngsters want to read about superheroes, and many are willing to forgo their iPods, Game Boys, Xboxes, and video games to do so. This is a cause for celebration in today's culture.

The action-oriented story lines found in most graphic novels serve to keep student interest high. Even a comic's "slow" times keep the kid's interest because the action is visual. A student *reads* the words, *sees* the action, *comprehends* the meaning, and is motivated to read more. It's an end that justifies the means.

Comics, due to monthly distribution, are on the cutting edge of pop culture; they react swiftly to social and cultural changes and address them in a timely fashion. Following the 9/11 terrorist attacks, TV programs were rescheduled and movie releases were delayed or aban-doned. It took book publishers and the music industry nearly a year to provide responses for the attacks. By contrast, the comic-book industry responded in less than a month with *Heroes* and *The Amazing Spider-Man.* The comic-book industry keeps its finger on the pulse of what is happening in the world, what kids view as "cool," and they respond to it with lightning speed. The industry's reward is more sales; society's reward is more student readers.

Can You Explain Why the Words "Anime," "*Bone*," and "Manga" Are Often Associated With Graphic Novels?

Anime: Anime is an art form that incorporates various aspects of Japanese culture. Anime is used in many comics and graphic novels, as well as on e-cards, wallpaper, fan art, wearing apparel, and video game songs.

Bone: Bone, a series of graphic novels published in the United States, is highly popular with middle and high school students. *Bone* graphic novels combine the humor and look of early Disney movies with the scope of the *Lord of the Rings.* The characters in *Bone* are both cute and scary, and every panel is infused with dynamic energy.

At age four, *Bone's* acclaimed creator, Jeff Smith, began drawing the characters that eventually would populate his series. Smith remembers looking forward to Sunday mornings when his father would read him the *Peanuts* comic strip. Smith wanted to learn to read so that he didn't have to wait for his dad to wake up in order to find out what Snoopy and Charlie Brown were saying in those little bubbles—and he did. To this day Smith credits *Peanuts* as his inspiration to read, and now his *Bone* series is hooking a new generation of readers.

Manga: Manga (pronounced "mah-n-gah") is an art form. The term is commonly used as a label for the Japanese print comic that is so wildly popular in the United States, particularly among preteen and teenage girls. Most manga books read from back to front, but this format does not seem to confuse kids. Most manga characters have exaggerated eyes, simplified features, and straight "spiked" hair. Manga is known for its highly stylized and intricate artwork and, unlike American comics that concentrate on superhero fantasy adventures, manga spans a wide range of topics. Cat Turner, a secondary English specialist and teacher at Henry Wise Wood High School in Calgary, Alberta, said, "Manga is very popular with our students, so much so that many students are actually learning Japanese so that they can read the newest manga straight off the press, instead of waiting for translations." It's hard to fault that kind of result.

Manga does, however, come with a red flag that American educators, media specialists, and librarians need to be aware of. Because manga is translated from comics originally published in Japan, the stories reflect their culture of origin—a situation that is sometimes at odds with mainstream culture in the United States. A prime example is the prevalence of incidental, partial nudity and raunchy humor found in many titles published for young Japanese and Korean readers. For example, *Ranma ½* and *Dragon Ball Z* are two titles for younger readers in Japan. In the United States, librarians put these books in the Young Adult or Adult sections because they include what our culture considers to be adult situations. School librarians can feel more secure about selecting manga for their collections if they look at the suggested reader level listed on the book and ratchet it up a notch. If a manga's cover lists a recommended age of 13+, teachers and media specialists may want to withhold it from their school's collection, or reserve it for high school juniors and seniors.

What Is the Difference Between a Comic Book and a Graphic Novel?

The differences between comic books and graphic novels are slim. Most of us think of the comic book as a stapled booklet similar to a magazine; 28 pages of text and graphics enclosed in panels, published monthly, and inexpensive. This type of periodical remains in existence and retains its popularity, but the term "comic book" has evolved. Today the term "comic book" describes any *format* that uses a combination of frames, words, and pictures to convey meaning and tell a story. Perhaps it will help us understand the distinction between the two if we remember that *all graphic novels are comic books, but not all comic books are graphic novels.* Every publication that uses the format of frames surrounding text and graphics is considered a comic or a comic book. The lengthy ones, referred to as graphic novels, are also comics. Think of it this way. When John Doe receives his doctoral degree he becomes Dr. Doe—but he is still John. When the comic book exceeds 50 pages (roughly) and is bound in a soft or hard cover, it becomes a graphic novel—but it is still a comic.

Should Classrooms and Media Centers Develop and Maintain Collections for Both Comics and Graphic Novels?

Maintaining separate collections is not recommended. A comic book consisting of 28 pages costs a school about $2.40, is not durable, and (due to size and flexibility) is a prime target for theft. This creates a significant challenge to those responsible for maintaining a circulating collection. That being said, I suggest developing a non-circulating collection, and inviting students to bring their own personal copies of age- and content-appropriate comic books to school to read in their "free" time. Graphic novels are bound like traditional books and last longer than a comic book. These longer pieces are favorites with teachers because graphic novels can be incorporated into the curriculum and used as springboards for class projects.

Most Kids Are Wild About Graphic Novels.
Is That Why Some Teachers Use Them
and Others Are Thinking About It?

Although the popularity of comic books and graphic novels may be the catalyst that prompts educators to investigate the medium, those who ultimately decide to use them for instruction do so because of their value. Teachers use graphic novels because they *enable* the struggling reader, *motivate* the reluctant one, and *challenge* the high-level learner.

Many struggling readers (kids who read below grade level) are unable to visualize pictures in their heads. They cannot "see" in their minds what is happening in the text, and consequently they do not comprehend the text's message. For these kids, reading is a mandated task of decoding letters—devoid of meaning, without pleasure, and something to avoid. They have grown up with TV, electronic games, video games, and graphic software, and they *need* graphics to help them understand the message. The graphic novel satisfies this need.

Reluctant readers are students between seven and sixteen who can read, but don't. These kids read only if their interest is piqued and if they are allowed to read something they enjoy. Again, the graphic novel meets their need.

Obviously, high-level readers can and do utilize in-depth and challenging texts. The graphic novel meets the needs of the high-level reader when it is combined with an artistic endeavor, is used as a springboard for a writing activity, or serves as an introduction to the comic's classic counterpart.

Are Teachers Caving In to Student
Demand When They Use Graphic Novels?

Perhaps, but common sense suggests that the end (struggling readers who learn to read, reluctant readers who enjoy reading, and high-achieving readers who expand their horizons) justifies the means. Furthermore, graphic novels do not have to be the "end." They can be a launch pad for something bigger farther down the road. It's important to remember that *we must make kids want to read before we can make them read what we want them to.* Mark Twain said, "The man who doesn't read is no better off than the man who can't read." Educators and librarians have an obligation to try to reach kids who don't read before they become adults who don't read.

Is "Enticing Kids to Read" Enough of a Reason to Put Graphic Novels Into our School Classrooms and Libraries?

Probably, but the benefit that comes from reading graphic novels extends beyond enticement. The reading of graphic novels promotes better reading skills, improves comprehension, and complements other areas of the curriculum. The student who, due to physiological, environmental, or cultural background, is unable to form pictures in his head while reading the printed word is not really reading. He is simply word-calling. The words give him no message, and they bring him no joy. He needs more.

The reduced amount of text and attention-grabbing graphics in graphic novels help ESL students and struggling readers infer, predict, and reflect on what they read. Their skills improve as they read more, their improved skills lead to greater comprehension, and their enhanced comprehension creates a desire to read more. It's a happy circle story that has no ending.

If this sounds too good to be true, introduce your students (fourth grade and above) to the graphic novel *Broken Sky*, a series of seven books, and see for yourself what they do for kids. Chris Wooding's (2000) *Broken Sky* books have the appearance of a chapter book, but the vocabulary (combined with the graphics) is manageable for kids who are stymied by "print-only" material. You've heard the phrase, "A picture is worth a thousand words." For kids who lack the ability to comprehend page after page of nothing but print, a graphic is worth more than a thousand words. A graphic novel can be the difference between failure and success, and that value is immeasurable.

I Understand the Value of Using Graphic Novels With Reluctant and Struggling Readers. Do They Offer Any Benefit for Proficient Readers Who Already Like to Read?

Graphic novels benefit all students, regardless of their reading skill or level of engagement. Both groups share some advantages, and both groups enjoy advantages that are unique to their achievement level. We'll look at the shared advantages first.

The stories in graphic novels are interesting and complex, and they appeal to kids at all reading levels. Each child reads, and each builds on his existing skills. Struggling readers improve, and advanced readers soar.

Graphic novels serve as an equalizer between academically achieving and struggling learners. A sense of unity develops and a spirit of camaraderie forms when kids share a common interest and a passion for what they are doing. Time and again we see this happen when graphic novels become a part of the classroom curriculum. An engaging discussion on *Teen Titans* (DC Comics, 1996) or a shared viewing of the film *Road to Perdition* starring Tom Hanks (based on the graphic novel *Road to Perdition,* Collins, 2002) creates bonds and forms friendships.

Advanced and engaged readers profit when the teacher combines the reading of graphic novels with the writing process. This multi-sensory activity stirs the imaginations of more advanced readers and challenges them to use their higher-level thinking, reading, and writing skills.

One reason teachers use graphic novels is to steer students toward more prose-oriented, "better" reading—including the classics. Consider Will Eisner's (2000) graphic novel *The Last Knight. The Last Knight* is a comical graphic novel (third- to fourth-grade reading level) that can be used to introduce readers to Miguel de Cervantes' classic character Don Quixote. Struggling and reluctant readers who are fans of knights in armor and slapstick humor can simply enjoy the silliness of *The Last Knight,* whereas high-level, engaged readers can move into its classic counterpart. Another example is the graphic novel *The Adventures of Tom Sawyer* (Twain & Hall, 2007). The appealing illustrations and the low readability level (second to third grade) of this graphic novel entice lower-level readers, and it propels high achievers into Mark Twain's classic work by the same title. *Treasure Island* (Stevenson & Hamilton, 2005), *Call of the Wild* (London & Kleid, 2006), *The Wizard of Oz* (Baum & Cavallaro, 2005), *The Red Badge of Courage* (Crane & Vansant, 2005), and *Robin Hood* (Shepard & Watson, 2006) are a few of the countless number of classics that have graphic-novel counterparts.

Some Girls Don't Like Graphic Novels. Do I Dare Use Them as Mandatory Reading, or Should They Be Strictly Voluntary?

It is true that some girls don't like graphic novels, but many do. The same can be said for some boys. No matter what we teach or how we present it, we will not simultaneously satisfy every student's learning style or suit every kid's taste. As we make decisions about what to teach and how to teach it, we need to consider the needs of many rather than the preferences of a few.

If you believe graphic novels have merit, then you are justified in making them part of your curriculum. Nobody, including this writer, recommends a full diet of graphic novels. They should be introduced to all students, used sporadically with the entire class, and be readily accessible for those who want more of them.

Do Graphic Novels Improve Reading Test Scores?

Although teachers who use them as one part of their literacy curriculum *think* they cause test scores to rise (because kids read more and their level of engagement is higher), to date there is little research to prove this assumption. Why not? Because the use of graphic novels in the classroom is still in its infancy. Nationwide, only 4 percent of fourth- through twelfth-grade teachers use graphic novels in their classrooms, and with the exception of Maryland, where a statewide usage program is being piloted, the option of using graphic novels is left primarily to each individual teacher. Perhaps, in the not-too-distant future, Maryland's pilot program, spearheaded by State Superintendent of Schools Nancy Grasmick, will provide data that will help educators decide whether or not graphic novels lead to higher scores.

Despite the lack of statistical evidence, graphic-novel proponents say graphic novels will cause test scores to rise because, in the words of Jim Trelease, "The more you read the better you get, the better you get at it, the more you like it; and the more you like it, the more you do it" (2001, p. 1). Children who struggle with or dislike reading don't read (except when forced to) and consequently they don't "get better." Conversely, the kid who gets hooked on reading—regardless of the means—seeks out more books, reads more, and gets better. Common sense tells us that if kids read better their scores will improve.

What Suggestions Do You Have for the Teacher, Librarian, or Media Specialist Who Wants to Start a Graphic Novel Collection?

Do what this writer did while researching this topic: consult experts in the industry. If you're thinking of starting a graphic-novel collection, visit your nearest comic book dealer. In a 2002 article written for the American Library Association, Steve Raitieri suggests making a personal visit to a comic shop, looking around, and asking a lot of questions. He goes on to say,

> Employees and owners of comic shops are likely to be long-time fans that love to talk about comics. They can be a great resource to help you find out what's good, what's popular, what's new and exciting, and what the "must have" classics are—and also what to avoid. It's also helpful to look at books before you buy them. Gain a sense of the different genres and styles that are available, and get an idea of what to expect from them. (Raitieri, 2002)

Another valuable resource for graphic novel selection is the large chain bookstore. Most chains have one or more comic book experts on staff who are willing to share their knowledge and expertise. I found my graphic novel expert, Zach Douglas, at a Barnes and Noble bookstore in Cedar Rapids, Iowa, and I will be forever indebted to him. If you inquire around a bit, I'm sure you'll find a "Zach" in your area, too.

Whether you are starting a collection or adding to one, you will want to consult some Web sites and reference books that offer lists of graphic novels categorized by grade level and topic. Several of these sites are listed at the end of this chapter. If you have a lot of time (highly doubtful) and are brave), you may want to do your own evaluating of graphic novels rather than rely on the advice or recommendations of others. If this is the case, check out the Brodart.com Web site, also listed at the end of this chapter. It is important to remember that Brodart's guidelines, as well as others you might use, are *general* in nature and will not fit every school or community. Be certain to keep your community's values and expectations in mind when purchasing graphic novels, and *never* purchase non-returnable books. Every time you receive a graphic novel order, examine each title carefully. If you are in doubt as to whether a particular comic is appropriate or not, err on the side of caution and send it back. Don't give nitpickers an opportunity to criticize your program.

You Have Talked About Using Graphic Novels With Middle and High School Students. Aren't There Any Available for the Younger Kids?

Yes, there are many such titles on the market. The "sidekicks for kids" section of the noflyingnotights.com Web site listed at the end of this chapter has a lengthy list of good intermediate graphic novel titles, with a review for each title.

Personal favorites for grades 3–5:

Amelia Rules: The Whole World's Crazy (Gownley, 2006). *Amelia Rules* is filled with hilarious adventures and tough lessons that all kids face as they grow up. Amelia, always laughing on the outside, cries inside as she struggles to cope with her parents' divorce, a new school, her nerdy reputation, and her rival—Ronda. *Amelia Rules* is an honest, straightforward, and very funny commentary on the art of growing up.

Scary Godmother (Thompson, 1997). Hannah Marie meets Scary Godmother one Halloween while her cousin Jimmy tries to scare her at the haunted house. Hannah Marie has fun with the Monster under the bed, a singing skeleton, a lazy werewolf, and a vampire who wants a friend to play with.

You Can't Take a Balloon Into the Metropolitan Museum (Weitzman, 1998). A little girl's errant balloon slips away from the museum guard and takes the reader on a wonderful romp through New York. This delightful, fantasy-filled wordless book is about the brilliant works of art located inside New York's Metropolitan Museum, and the famous "must not miss" tourist spots in the Big Apple.

Herobear and the Kid (Kunkel, 2002). In this story, ten-year-old Tyler inherits a broken pocket watch and a stuffed bear from his grandfather. Tyler is less than enthusiastic about his gifts until Herobear comes alive and needs help. Together Tyler and Herobear find adventure, fun, and a bit of danger. Boys love this one.

Tellos: Reluctant Heroes (Dezago, 2001). Students who like Harry Potter will love *Tellos*. It has honorable thieves, loyal companions, threatening adversaries, and a young boy destined to be a hero. And in the words of a juvenile Amazon.com reviewer, "The drawings are good and the inking is AWESOME."

I Want to Use Graphic Novels in My Seventh-Grade Class Next Year, but No One Else in Our District Uses Them. What Do You Suggest?

During coffee breaks, lunchtime, and afterschool chats, mention your plan to your teaching colleagues and media personnel. Explain how you think graphic novels would benefit your class and other students in the school as well. Present your plan with enthusiasm and avoid portraying yourself as the only dude cool enough to try innovative practices. *Welcome your colleagues' input*, proceed slowly, and when you sense the climate is right, encourage them to join you in the venture. The more team members you have, the better your chances are for winning.

Do your research, commit it to memory, and share your proposal with your principal *before* you initiate the program. Once the program begins you may encounter some resistance from staff, parents, or school board members. If this happens, you will need a friend in high places and that friend had better be the principal. Principals don't take kindly to being blind-sided with a complaint concerning an issue they were unaware of.

Be cautious about the titles you purchase. Avoiding books that contain sex, nudity, or violence will help protect your fledgling efforts from criticism. Consult the experts (discussed earlier in this chapter), find the right material for your audience, and preview everything you buy. If, after reviewing a purchased book, you think it *might* be objectionable to some—send it back. It's better to be safe than sorry.

Finally, market your product every chance you get. Volunteer to give graphic-novel book talks to PTA groups, the school board, service organizations, faculty meetings, and the like. Because graphic novels are relatively new, they are often regarded with skepticism. The more people you can introduce to the graphic novel and the more people who see your enthusiasm, the greater your success will be. Once you get John Q. Public on your side, you have it made. You needn't worry about how students will react to graphic novels because that's a given. They'll fight to check out the ones you have, and they'll clamor for more. I promise.

Can Graphic Novels Be Plugged Into the Existing Curriculum?

Age-appropriate graphic novels can be incorporated into some curriculum areas, but not all. Several titles are available for supplementing art, history, literature, music, mythology, science, and social issues units, whereas others are used primarily for getting struggling and reluctant readers into books or leading high achieving readers into more enriching endeavors.

The following list is a minute sampling of currently available graphic novels that are being used effectively in the various curricula strands and as motivational tools. I have (for lack of a better word) labeled the motivational category as "General." The titles listed below represent only the tip of the iceberg of what is out there. Thousands of worthwhile graphic novels are already in print, and new ones are being released every month. If you are planning to develop a classroom or media center collection of graphic novels, you will want to consult one or more of the references and Web sites listed at the end of this chapter.

Upper Elementary

Art:

Manga Mania: How to Draw Japanese Comics by Hart. Watson-Guptill (2000) Drawing

General:

Comic Adventures of Boots by Kitamura. St. Martin's Press (2002) Humorous fiction, cats

Marvel Masterworks: Daredevil by Lee. Marvel Books (2001) Daredevil, superheroes

Spirited Away by Miyazaki. Viz Communications (2002) Fantasy, action, magic

The Essential Uncanny X-Men by Lee. Marvel Comics (2003) Superheroes

Ultimate X-Men by Sanderson. DK (2000) Superheroes

Literature:

Cave In by Ralph. Highwater Books (1999) Children's stories, adventure

Climbing Out by Ralph. Brian Ralph (2003) Children's stories, animal stories

Courtney Crumin and the Night Things by Naifeh. Oni Press (2003) Fantasy

Leave It to Chance by Robinson. Image (2003) Fantasy, mystery, fiction

Speed Racer: Born to Race by Yune. DC Comics/Wildstorm (2000) Auto racing fiction

Thieves and Kings by Oakley. I Box. (2001) Magic, action and adventure, wizardry

Social Issues:

Good Bye, Chunky Rice by Thompson. Top Shelf Productions (2001) Adventure, friendship

Middle School

Art:

Anime Mania: How to Draw Characters for Japanese Animation by Hart. Watson-Guptill (2002)

General:

Amazing Spider-Man: Coming Home by Straczynski. Marvel Comics (2002) Superheroes

Batman: Hong Kong by Moench. DC Comics (2003) Superheroes

Girl Genius-Book by Foglio. Airship Entertainment (2003) Humorous fiction, romance

Mad About Super Heroes by Meglin. DC Comics (2002) Superheroes

Samurai Noir by Oeming. Image Comics (2003) Martial arts, fiction

Storm Riders Volume I by Ma. Comics One (2002) Swords and sorcery, martial arts

Zero Girl by Kieth. DC Comics (2001) Humor, love stories, fiction

History:

Barnum by Chaykin. DC Comics (2003) Circus, comics, American history

Jack the Ripper by Geary. NBM (2003) History, biography, true crime

The Cartoon History of the Universe by Gonick. Doubleday (2002) History, ancient history

The Fatal Bullet: The Assassination of President Garfield by Geary. NBM (2003) American history

Literature:

Crystal Ball by Rucka. Oni Press (2003) Mystery, espionage, fiction

Delicate Creatures by Straczynski. Image Comics (2001) Fantasy, folk and fairy tales

Herobear and the Kid: Volume 1, Inheritance by Kunkel. Astonish Comics (2003) Fantasy

Music:

Days Like This by Torres. Oni Press (2003) Music, fiction, girls' stories

Strum & Drang: Great Moments in Rock & Roll by Orff. Alternative Comics (2003)

Science:

Dignifying Science by Ottaviani et al. G.T. Labs (2000) Science, biography

Fallout by Ottaviani et al. G.T. Labs (2001) Nuclear science, biography, humorous fiction

Metropolis by Tezuka. Dark Horse (2003) Science fiction and fantasy

Red Rocket 7 by Allred. Dark Horse (1998) Science fiction and fantasy

Shadow Star Volume I by Kitoh. Dark Horse (2001)

Usagi Yojimbo: Grasscutter & Journey to Atsuta Shrine by Sakai. Dark Horse (2002) Science fiction

Social Issues:

9-11: Stories to Remember by various authors. DC Comics (2002).

Amy Unbounded: Belondweg Blossoming by Hartman. Pug House (2003) Coming-of-age

Fagin the Jew by Eisner. Doubleday (2003) Racism, Jewish life, fiction

Hopeless Savages by Van Meter. Oni Press (2003) Humorous fiction, teenagers, families

King Volume I by Anderson. Fantagraphics (1994) Martin Luther King Jr., biography

Pedro and Me by Winick. Henry Holt (2000)

Persepolis by Satrapi. Pantheon (2003) Adolescent stories, growing up, biography

High School
General:

The Adventures of Barry Ween, Boy Genius by Winick. Oni Press (1999) Humorous fiction

Catch as Catch Can by Cook. Highwater Books (1999) Humorous fiction

Daredevil: Underboss by Bendis. Marvel Books (2002) Daredevil, superheroes

Rebound, Volume I by Nishiyama. Tokyopop (2003) Basketball, humor, drama

Health:

The Cartoon Guide to Sex by Gonick and DeVault. Harperperennial Library (1999)

History:

Berlin by Lutes. Drawn & Quarterly. (2002) Life of citizens of Berlin between World War I and World War II

Fallout by Ottaviani. (2001) The political science of the atomic bomb

Fax From Sarajevo by Kubert. Dark Horse Comics (1998) Modern war, Yugoslavia, biography

From Hell by Moore and Campbell. Campbell Comics (2000) World history–England, true crime

Maus: A Survivor's Tale by Spiegelman. Pantheon (1997) The Holocaust

Yossel, April 19, 1943 by Kubert. ibooks (2003) World War II, Warsaw Ghetto uprising

Literature:

Graphic Classics: Volume I. Edited by Pomplun. (2004) Twelve Edgar Allen Poe fables

Music:

> *Great Moments in Rock & Roll* by Orff. (2005) Rock and roll music

Political Science:

> *Notes from a Defeatist* by Sacco. Fantagraphics (2003) War, political science, social studies
>
> *Palestine* by Sacco. Fantagraphics (2002) Political science, social studies
>
> *Safe Area Gorazed* by Sacco. Fantagraphics (2000) War, Bosnia, ethnic cleansing

Science:

> *Dignifying Science* by Ottaviani et al. G.T. Labs (2000) Science, biography
>
> *Onegai Teacher* by Seto. ComicsOne (2003) Fantasy, manga, science fiction

Social Issues:

> *9-11 Emergency Relief* by Mason et al. Alternative Comics (2002)
>
> *I Never Liked You* by Brown. Drawn & Quarterly (2001) Relationships, biography
>
> *The Barefoot Serpent* by Kurosawa. Top Shelf Productions (2003) Family, grief, suicide

I Want to Purchase a Few Graphic Novels to "Test the Water" With My Seventh-Grade Class. The Administration Supports My Plan, but They Lack the Funds to Finance It. Suggestions?

First, try to get one or more colleagues to jump on your ship; there's strength in numbers. Second, beg, borrow, or steal (just kidding) a graphic novel that you think your students will like and introduce it with a book talk. An age-appropriate superhero comic works well for this endeavor. Develop a mini-unit to correlate with your book, keeping in mind that you are trying to generate enthusiasm among your students. Plan a Graphic Reading Night (described below) as a culminating activity, and invite the parents.

Your Graphic Reading Night will, of course, focus on the students. They should wear a costume that correlates with the book, greet the parents, put on the "program," and serve refreshments. During the informal socialization period following the program, go to the front of the room and make your pitch.

After you thank them for coming and brag about their kids a bit, give a *short* sales pitch on the value of the graphic novel and explain the lack of available funds. Casually (ahem) mention that if anyone would like to donate money to purchase a book, it would be appreciated.

During my long tenure in the classroom I used this approach on a few occasions (always with the principal's permission), and invariably I got a favorable response. Parents want to support their child's learning endeavors, and those who can afford to will do so—if they understand the need. Who will be your biggest benefactor? Grandparents. Most grandparents have a few discretionary bucks to spend, and nearly all want to do what they can to help their grandkids. Be sure you invite them to your Graphic Reading Night celebration; their input will fatten your graphic-novel piggy bank.

What Titles Do You Recommend for Each Grade Level?

There are thousands of graphic novels in print, and hundreds more are being published each year. A comprehensive list of the good ones goes far beyond the scope of this chapter. Furthermore, by the time these words reach print, the list would be outdated. Because of these reasons I am recommending several Web sites where, with the click of a mouse, you can find weekly updated lists that will give you the information you need.

The following list is the work of Mike Quinn, reference specialist at the Ames, Iowa Public Library. All of the Web sites listed are excellent, and the one that heads the list is awesome.

Web Sites to Get You Started and Keep You Current:

http://www.noflyingnotights.com

> Reviews graphic novels for kids, teens, and young adults. This is an excellent site for the novice who is starting (or thinking about starting) a graphic-novel collection.

http://my.voyager.net/~sraiteri/graphicnovels.htm

> Includes recommendations for a basic graphic-novel collection. Information gathered and presented by Steve Raitieri, a librarian from Xenia, Ohio.

http://ublib.buffalo.edu/lml/comics/pages/do-comics.html

> Another Raitieri-managed site. This one has links to comic book and graphic-novel sites that provide recommended and black-balled title lists.

http://bookshelf.diamondcomics.com/

> Diamond Comics distributors' link to a special page for librarians and educators. Has useful information for the graphic-novel novice.

http://www.graphicnovels.brodart.com/selection_criteria.htm

> Guidelines for starting or building a graphic-novel collection. Recommendations are categorized by age and grade level.

http://www.tascorp.org/section/what_we_do/program_support/academic/literacy/comic

> Michael Bitz's Comic Book Project

www.readwritethink.org

> Teacher's lesson plan for combining music with the graphic novel: "Examining Transcendentalism Through Popular Culture."

http://www.nyccomicbookmuseum.org/education/education.htm

> Home page of the New York City Comic Book Museum. Has useful suggestions for incorporating writing and art activities into the comic book enhanced curriculum. Click on "Back to the Drawing Board: Once-Banned Comic Books Now a Teaching Tool," and let your imagination roll.

Do You Have Any Additional Suggestions?

Finding the time to use graphic novels is a concern for every teacher. Teachers rarely have extra hours (or even minutes) to spare. Something must be eliminated before something new can be added. Discuss this issue with your colleagues and administrators and try to reach consensus on which book or activity can be dropped—at least on a trial basis—as you try this "new" approach.

Stock your study halls, homerooms, and cafeteria with an ample supply of "on-site only" graphic novels. Do not allow these books to be taken from the room where they are housed.

Take five minutes off each period of the day and combine them into an end-of-the-day, *everyday*, recreational reading period. This "Relax and

Read" portion of the day should be mandatory, but not unpleasant. Let students read what they want (as long as it isn't morally objectionable), and where they want—within reason. Does this plan have drawbacks? Sure. Will the benefits outweigh the hassles? Absolutely. Most of today's kids read nothing beyond that which is required, and some don't even do that. If we really want to get students reading, we must allot part of the school day for reading and allow kids to read the kinds of books they enjoy.

Spearhead an afterschool graphic book club. Two six-week sessions (one in the fall and the other in the spring) seem to work well. Club members pick the novel they want to read, and they take turns bringing afterschool snacks. The facilitator (you) should try to arrange one or two fun activities to associate with each book. A school near where I live often culminates their six-week session with a prearranged conference telephone call between the book's author and club members. It's a magical thing to see the look on a kid's face as he talks to a "real" author on the phone. If you see it, you won't forget it. And better yet—you'll no longer care about not getting paid for your facilitating role because you will already have received your reward.

Final Thoughts

According to a 2004 National Endowment for the Arts (NEA) survey, *Reading at Risk: A Survey of Literary Reading in America* (2004), literary reading is in dramatic decline. The study reported drops in all groups studied, with the steepest rate of decline—28 percent—occurring in the youngest age groups. Although this information is disturbing, it is not surprising.

Today's students have grown up with TV, Game Boys, electronic "learning" devices, computer programs that whistle and toot, and other devices that are accompanied by graphics and offer instant gratification. A lot of children don't like to read, and many of them won't read, unless we meet them on their own turf and teach them the way they learn—some of the time.

Most kids enjoy graphic novels, and most profit from them. I urge you to give them a try. When you see your students fighting over who gets to be the first one to check out the latest release, you'll be glad you did.

Reference Material for Additional Study
(Courtesy of Mike Quinn of the Ames, IA Public Library):

Gorman, Michele. *Getting Graphic! Using Graphic Novels to Promote Literacy with Preteens and Teens*. Worthington, OH: Linworth Publishing, 2003.

Lyga, Allyson A. W. and Barry Lyga. *Graphic Novels in Your Media Center: A Definitive Guide*. Westport, CT: Libraries Unlimited, 2004. If you are thinking about taking a plunge into the pool of graphic novels, you'll want to check this one out.

McCloud, Scott. *Understanding Comics.* Northampton, MA: Tundra Publishing, 1993. An outstanding analysis of what a comic is and how it works.

Miller, Steve. *Developing and Promoting Graphic Novel Collections.* New York: Neal Schuman Publishers, 2005. A good introduction for building a collection.

Weiner, Stephen. *Faster Than a Speeding Bullet: The Rise of the Graphic Novel.* New York: NBM Publishing, 2003. History of the comic. (Not useful for starting or building a collection.)

Weiner, Stephen. *The 101 Best Graphic Novels.* New York: NBM Publishing 2001. An excellent source for starting a new collection.

Wright, Bradford W. *Comic Book Nation: The Transformation of Youth Culture in America.* Baltimore: Johns Hopkins University Press, 2001. Helpful information to use when "presenting your case" to skeptics.

REFERENCES

Baum, F. L., & Cavallaro, M. (2005). *The wizard of Oz: The graphic novel.* New York: Puffin.

Collins, M. A. (2002). *Road to perdition.* New York: Pocket.

Crane, S., & Vansant, W. (2005). *The red badge of courage: The graphic novel.* New York: Puffin.

Dezago, T. (2001). *Tellos: Reluctant heroes.* Berkeley, CA: Image Comics.

Eisner, W. (2000). *The last knight: An introduction to Don Quixote by Miguel de Cervantes.* New York: NBM.

Gownley, J. (2006). *Amelia rules! The whole world's crazy.* Renaissance Press.

Kunkel, M. (2002). *Herobear and the kid.* Toluca Lake, CA: Astonish.

London, J., & Kleid, N. (2006). *Call of the wild: The graphic novel.* New York: Puffin.

McKeaver, S. & Green, R. (1996). *Teen titans.* New York: DC Comics.

McTaggart, J. (2003). *From the teacher's desk.* Booklocker.

National Endowment for the Arts. (2004). *Reading at risk: A survey of literary reading in America.* Washington, DC: Author.

Raitieri, S. (2002). Graphic novel collection development. Retrieved December 19, 2006, from http://www.ala.org/ala/yalsa/teenreading/trw/trw2002/collectiondevelopment.htm

Shepard, A., & Watson, A. L. (2006). *Robin Hood.* Minneapolis, MN: Stone Arch.

Smith, J. (2005). *Bone.* New York: Graphix/Scholastic.

Stevenson, R. L., & Hamilton, T. (2005). *Treasure Island: The graphic novel.* New York: Puffin.

Thompson, J. (1997). *Scary godmother.* San Antonio, TX: Sirius.

Trelease, J. (2001). *The read aloud handbook* (5th ed.). New York: Penguin.

Twain, M., & Hall, M. C. (2007). *The adventures of Tom Sawyer.* Minneapolis, MN: Stone Arch.

Weitzman, J. P. (1998). *You can't take a balloon into the Metropolitan Museum.* New York: Dial.

Wooding, C. (2000). *Broken sky.* New York: Scholastic.

3

Comics, the Canon, and the Classroom

James Bucky Carter

What might explain the resistance to the use of graphic novels, comics, and other visual literacy tools in classrooms? Carter offers a provocative theory—that policies and practices influence what is left out of curriculum. Further, Carter asserts that this may stem from deeply submerged notions about what constitutes school-based literacy.

Teachers need to find a place in their classrooms for comic books and graphic novels because it is sound practice to do so. Yet, to date, the case for the educational utility of these forms of sequential art is still being made. This chapter explores the possible hidden ramifications of teachers' reluctance to embrace the visual media of comics and graphic novels into the classroom and suggests that integrating them is a step toward a realization of more democratic notions of text, literacy, and curriculum. The existence of literary canons and teachers' purposeful or inadvertent propagation of them are seen as probable reasons why comics and graphic novels have yet to be properly integrated and acknowledged in education, and it is suggested that by viewing the canon as an evolving force, teachers can be empowered to embrace sequential art forms and elude the effects of elitist thinking that might have kept comics and graphic novels at bay for so long.

MIXING WORDS AND IMAGES

The research suggesting that mixing words and images (what most comics and graphic novels do skillfully) is a great way to foster comprehension and memory skills is bountiful. Thomas G. Gunning (2005) illuminated key research in this area in his excellent text *Creating Literacy Instruction for All Students*. Schnorr and Atkinson (1969) observed that encoding words visually helps students remember twice as many words as those who only encode verbally. Gambrell and Bales (1986) found that comprehension among students increased after only thirty minutes of imaging instruction. Maria (1990) realized that, with some training in visualization and some effective prompting, her fourth-graders were able to enrich their comprehension of the story based on their artwork. As well, she noted that otherwise reserved students began to contribute to discussions. Gunning (2005) observed, "Creating images serves three functions: fostering understanding, retaining information, and monitoring for meaning. . . . [it] can also be used as a pictorial summary" (p. 301) and he recommends direct teaching of imaging as a strategy. Duke and Pearson reiterated Gunning's claims: "There is an old saying that a picture is worth a thousand words. When it comes to comprehension, this saying might be paraphrased, 'a visual display helps readers understand, organize, and remember some of those thousand words'" (as cited in Farstrup & Samuels, 2002, p. 218). Indeed, there is an entire theory built around the idea that schema can be stored both verbally and visually. Dual Coding Theory, or DCT (Clark & Paivio, 1991; Paivio, 1986; Sadoski & Paivio, 1991), continues to have a major impact on cognitive psychology and education.

There is also contemporary research and current practice that directly illuminates the utility of comics and graphic novels in the classroom. Smith and Wilhelm (2002) have demonstrated via their longitudinal study into the reading habits of young men that graphic novels are one of the few media able to hold their interest. Michael Bitz's work with the Comic Book Project has given hundreds of students the skills to compose compelling narratives via the comic book format. Some of the impressive results of their labors are easily accessed and viewed at *http://www.comicbook project.org*. Cary's *Going Graphic: Comics at Work in the Multilingual Classroom* (2004), in addition to giving some excellent and tested ideas for using sequential art in the classroom, details recent brain-based research that supports a focus on visualization. Krashen (2004) and Xu (2005) have recently published works in which teachers, students, and influential people give positive testimonials about their experiences working with or reading comics. Both Krashen and Cary give a run-down of some of the most compelling comics-related research of recent decades, including studies that suggest that reading comics can act as a gateway to more varied reading. Indeed, Krashen shows that the comics-education connection is almost as old as superhero comics themselves. In 1941, a mere three years after Superman's debut, Thorndike recommended that, "In view of the need of the upper elementary school and junior high school pupil for a large volume of reading and vocabulary experience, this source [comics] should not be neglected" (as cited in Krashen, 2004, p. 97).

Despite sixty years of comic-related research and advocacy, Cary (2004) admitted that "some educators still believe that comics retard rather than aid language development" (p. 30). Indeed, he says that while he has seen an increase in "comics-friendly teachers" over the last twelve years, "comics-*using* teachers have remained scarce" (p. 2). It seems that while most teachers understand that concept maps, word webs, graphs, and flowcharts are good for reading and remembering and a host of other valuable cognitive skills, sequential art (which also utilizes visual information) is rarely seen in the same light. As I often say to my teacher-education students: Words, letters, drawings, lines—they're all just graphemes, after all. Any visualization, whether it is made up of pictographs we recognize as drawings, or drawings we've come to recognize as letters, must be interpreted, coded, and comprehended by the mind of the one who views it. I see these acts as necessary for reading, but perhaps the idea of reading pictures is still too unfamiliar for many teachers to accept.

VISUAL LITERACY IN THE CLASSROOM: HARD TO SWALLOW OR A CASE OF POLITICAL INDIGESTION?

Why teachers have been so reluctant to embrace comics and graphic novels—media that already allow for these things and are representative of others' interpreting, understanding, monitoring, summarizing—is, to me, a great enigma. When we know visuals and visualizing are so beneficial, why, usually sometime after fourth grade or so, do we give up on good practice, instead deciding that getting our kids to read text-heavy chapter books should be our singular goal?

There may be many reasons why comics and graphic novels are still not helping as many students as they could. One could be ignorance. It is possible that teachers simply do not know enough about comics-related research and visualization as a literacy skill. It is also possible that many teachers don't possess a schema that connects "comic books" or "graphic novels" with learning. If lack of knowledge is not the culprit, perhaps there is still fallout from Frederic Wertham's *Seduction of the Innocent* (1954), which suggested a correlation between reading comics and an increase in adolescent violence and maladjustment, but this seems unlikely. Krashen (2004) has adequately shown that Wertham's claims have not been supported over time (p. 97).

As of yet, comics-related research has not been widely tested on graphic novels *as* graphic novels. Articles specifically addressing graphic novels' pedagogical potentiality have just begun to enter the field over the last decade or so, and books are few, but that is changing. Michele Gorman's *Getting Graphic: Using Graphic Novels to Promote Literacy With Preteens and Teens* (2003) and Stephen Weiner's *The 101 Best Graphic Novels* (2001) each offer scores of suggestions for age-appropriate graphic novels. Though it is probably safe to assume that research that deals with comic books applies directly to works that are essentially larger, generally more mature versions of comics, graphic novels have been in the American consciousness for only about thirty years now, and in teachers' consciousness for considerably less time, whereas their pamphlet-style cousins, comic books, have a longer tenure. Their "newness" may be part of what is keeping graphic novels out of many classrooms. There are forthcoming books that should help remedy this, such as an *MLA Approaches* volume and *Building Literacy Connections with Graphic Novels: Page by Page, Panel by Panel* (Carter, 2007), an edited volume in which contributors share ideas for using graphic novels in thematic units and with more traditional school texts such as *The Scarlet Letter, The Inferno, Beowulf,* and *Oliver Twist* in approaches I define roughly as "augmental" or "supplemental" in nature. An augmental approach describes the use of graphic novels to increase the number of texts from which teachers and students can sample in the classroom. In this approach, graphic novels are given equal billing with traditional classics. In contrast, teachers using a supplemental approach use graphic novels as secondary texts to more accepted or canonical texts (Carter, 2007).

Graphic Novel–Specific Articles of Note

Brenner, R. (March/April 2006). Graphic novels 101. FAQ. *The Horn Book Magazine*, 123–125.

Bucher, K. T., & Manning, M. L. (2004). Bringing graphic novels into a school's curriculum. *Clearinghouse, 78*(2), 67–72.

Esquivel, I. (2006). Graphic novels: A medium with momentum. *Journal of Media Literacy, 53*(2), 33–39.

Frey, N., & Fisher, D. (2004). Using graphic novels, anime, and the Internet in an urban high school. *English Journal, 93*(3), 19–25.

Rudiger, H. M. (March/April 2006). Reading lessons: Graphic novels 101. *The Hornbook Magazine*, 126–134.

Schwarz, G. (2006). Expanding literacies through graphic novels. *English Journal, 95*(6), 58–64.

Weiner, S. (2004). Show, don't tell: Graphic novels in the classroom. *English Journal, 94*(2), 114–117.

Of course, more research and teacher testimonials are needed to help teachers feel comfortable using graphic novels. To address the latter need, I ask you to consider how Tracey Saxon, a veteran middle school teacher, uses a classic graphic novel in her classroom:

> There are several ways that I incorporate the Pulitzer Prize winning graphic novel *Maus* (Spiegelman, 1993) into my Social Studies and English curricula. I have found the book to be a key component in engaging student interest. Students who were reluctant to read the normal text found the novel accessible and students who were able to read and understand the textbook found the novel interesting. My goal is to connect the past to the current existence of my students and *Maus* helps me meet them on a level that is both academically appropriate and culturally relevant.

Social Studies:

The Holocaust can be a daunting subject to teach to students who are overwhelmed by the sheer enormity of the event. By looking at the story of Vladek Spiegelman [Art's father and the main character of the book, which is the author's attempt to make sense of his family history and share their incredible stories], students are given perspective and can relate to the events by seeing them impact this one man and his friends. By getting to know the characters in the story, the events make an impression on the students.

Conflict is one of the main concepts that I teach in social studies, and conflict is represented on many levels in *Maus.* I have asked students to read the novel and keep a running list of the conflicts that they see in the book. They are asked to re-read the story and make lists of supporting lines and excerpts that define the players in the conflict. The lists range as student abilities range—but all can clearly see the literal cat versus mouse conflict and the conflict that exists between the Jews and the Nazis. Most of my students on all levels identify the conflict between Vladek and his second wife, Mala, and many also see the internal conflict that lives within Artie, the son, as he learns how to deal with his father. Further examination of the novel shows more than these conflicts, however, and I gain valuable insight to the prior knowledge of my students as they share details that they pick up while reading. One student with a strong background in art remarked that there is a definite difference in the way that the artist draws the cats and mice: the features of the mice are much more detailed than those of the cats. He wrote a paper, citing specific pages and drawings, that supported his theory that the artist clearly showed bias in his illustrations. While the concept was simple enough, the student was able to really examine the work and showcase where the mice were drawn (even as far as the Star of David on their jackets) with rounded lines and edges while the cats' lines were more severe and jagged. Another child explained the frailty of the condition of the Jews in the novel by noting their appearance (eyeglasses, small build, simple dress) in the illustrations of the mice.

I have also used the text to teach geography and I asked the students to follow Vladek's travels throughout the text. On the back of the novel there is a map of Poland and the neighboring countries in the area. I have made a map for students and had them make a travel diary, showing the different places Vladek went during the story. We add geographical features and make postcards based on the descriptions. It also helps us learn about the harsh conditions of the camps by writing about the various jobs that would need to be performed by prisoners in order to make the camp run.

English:
    In English, I explore the whole concept of "storyboarding" to help instill an appreciation of the graphic-novel form and to reinforce coherent writing by asking students to consider the many panels from *Maus* as storyboards. Students can see the story unfold by pictures and with words, and sometimes I ask them to rewrite the word balloons in the novel with their own words. I have found that my students construct written work of a much higher quality when they use the storyboard technique to develop a sequence to their own words and story. Since *Maus* is in black and white, and the drawings are effective but not too refined, my students can imitate the style and create their own graphic novels. Often the pictures and drawings help them to add details to their writing and I am convinced that they are the better writers from the experience. (T. Saxon, personal communication, December 12, 2005)

Tracey's findings and experiences reflect many of those found in the sources mentioned above. My own use of comics to help teach plot, character, vocabulary, writing, and comprehension in middle and high school classes have helped to create a richness in my classes that Tracey and her students certainly tap into. The medium just seems to have an innate ability to draw out new talents and give students new ways of interacting with traditional English/Language Arts concepts and materials. Why, then, does Cary (2004) lament over the lack of use by teachers?

A Matter of Policy?

If the reluctance to embrace comics and graphic novels does not stem from a lack of knowledge or novelty, one might view teachers' resistance as a policy position. Perhaps teachers feel that parents or administrators might take issue with these texts and enact policy to censor them. Indeed, I have experienced this myself when a central office administrator denied my request to teach *Maus* to a group of gifted eighth-graders, despite my principal's approval (Carter, 2007). If only I had known Tracey then! Or perhaps national policies stressing high-stakes testing have influenced teachers to ignore sequential art narratives and various types of literacy in favor of more traditional forms of print and literacy.

If there are policies that deter teachers from using comics and graphic novels, there are political reasons to use visual media in the classroom, as well. As teachers, even if it makes us uncomfortable to admit it, we are politicians and policy makers, too. We make policy in our classrooms and carry out policies from other agents. In every choice we make, in every word we say, we bring our values to bear (Apple, 1987; Freire, 1970; Postman & Wiengartner, 1969). If we find ourselves refusing to accept comics and graphic novels in our classrooms, or intentionally ignoring their potential, we are in reality making powerful political statements. These statements might suggest that we do not care much for others who think, read, and decode differently from the narrowest notion of reading and literacy.

Some classic research suggests that underrepresented and underprivileged cultures, even the functionally illiterate, are in actuality far from illiterate and do possess strong visual and language skills. Purcell-Gates (2001) described how Jenny, a mother who wants to learn to read print to help her son with his schoolwork, can sometimes pick up needed groceries based on the shapes and colors of the packaging. Though Purcell-Gates stated, "We do not learn to read and write speech. We learn to read and write written text" (p. 405), it is obvious that Jenny is reading in a broader sense that fits the visual or visual-kinesthetic intelligence (Gardner, 1983, 1993). She's coding as best she can with the literacy skills she has. These skills are not sufficient for print-based literacy, of course, but they do offer an important skill set worthy of acceptance and respect.

Heath (1983) noted that black children in Trackton, a pseudonym for a community in South Carolina that she observed for over a decade, grew up in a verbally rich environment. Speech was tied to status and young people constantly negotiated their place in the community and among peer groups via rhymes, elaborate stories, and verbal and kinesthetic posturing. What was problematic is that the visual-kinesthetic decoding competencies in which they were immersed were undervalued in their school culture.

Paulo Freire (1973) worked with print-illiterate peasants in South America by integrating authentic drawings into their discussions of their daily life, then slowly adding words to the illustration (for example, "brick" might be represented in the shape of a brick or bricks, or a poem might be written inside an illustration of a book of poetry). His students, mostly adults steeped in their powerless culture, were able to come to, as he says, read the word and the world. Freire's literacy is a critical literacy, and though there are many other proponents of critical pedagogy and the New

Literacies it embraces, it may be true that the current political climate does not make it easy for teachers to embrace critical ideas, which, as Freire, Heath, and Purcell-Gates illustrate, often emphasize that visual literacy and print literacy are highly intertwined, especially when we recognize that our culture is far from homogenous. But "teaching is political, and so, then, is teacher's knowledge" (DeBlase, 2007, p. 119), and it must be made clear that teachers are not hapless victims of political circumstance but are active policy players. Teachers' choices, the value decisions they make and the interpretations of policy they enact, are of great import in relation to the quality and equity of students' schooling experience.

Making Policy Equals Making Statements

In my opinion, to *choose* not to recognize the importance of visual literacy and students' visual cultures and to not make efforts to incorporate these elements into the classroom, for any reason, makes a very powerful political statement. The statement reads: "I support racist, elitist, and classist notions and policies of literature and education." It is a strong assertion, but racism, elitism, and classism have had a strong presence in the American classroom for generations. Perhaps the racism is what King calls dysconscious racism, "a limited and distorted view of racism that fails to take into account how inequality is created and perpetuated by the very structures of schools and society that these teachers generally believe promote equality" (as cited in Nieto, 2002, p. 230). But it is racism just the same. We could extend King's idea to *dysconscious classism* or *dysconscious elitism,* I suppose, as racism often rides the undertow of these two constructs. Certainly comic books have floundered under classism and elitism and the racism inherent therein. Heer and Worcester's *Arguing Comics: Literary Masters on a Popular Medium* (2004) reprints examples of comics criticism from throughout the twentieth century, many following the tone set by early writers who saw comics as

> symptomatic of much that was going wrong in the contemporary world: the newfound preference for visual stimulations rather than time-honored literary values; the growing strength of disorderly immigrant cultures in the United States which threatened to overturn Anglo-Saxon supremacy; the increasing acceptance of roughhouse slang which endangered norms of proper grammar and refined diction. (Heer & Worcester, 2004, p. 1)

Comics scholars have named this elitism as such and have examined the connections among racism, elitism, and classism in America's relationships to its comics (Wright, 2001). We might see the clash of ideas inherent in those who are critical of comics and those who accept them as analogous to the distinctions between those who support a stringent notion of cultural literacy and those who acknowledge the need for a critical literacy. As Cadiero-Kaplan (2002) pointed out, cultural literacy proponents believe that "there is specific cultural knowledge that 'all Americans need to know' to be competent citizens," and these proponents "assume that this knowledge is part of the upper-middle-class culture. As a result, those from lower socioeconomic classes or ethnically diverse groups must learn this knowledge to be successful in school" (p. 375).

To me, the elitism, classism, and smoldering racism of this line of thinking are obvious. Critical literacy advocates are much more open to non-traditional ideas of literacy that embrace home cultures and skill sets and focus more on creating and critiquing knowledge and discourse rather than finding it in a given set of texts or sources. Cultural literacy proponents are likely to accept a literary canon, whereas critical literacy proponents might call for an expansion of what makes a text suitable for study.

Following Canons as Deleterious Policy Decision

I assert that the construct of a literary canon as it has been interpreted as policy in schools constitutes a prime example of the racism, elitism, and classism that hinders visual literacy and visual materials such as comics and graphic novels from occupying a greater space in the classroom. Even if these canons have been created or reinforced by national policies, teachers, too, are policy makers in how they deal with these concepts and must see themselves as policy enactors. Examination of the literary canon reveals very little of the "dysconscious." Yet, in a rough examination of its history, it is evident that even something as stodgy as the canon can evolve. This is what teachers do when acknowledging aspects of visual literacy: they evolve their own canons.

Canons to the Fore! A Call for Action

The augmental and supplemental approaches to integrating comics and graphic novels into the curriculum mentioned earlier are essentially methods for expanding the literary canon. There are those who say the canon is dead, but in many classrooms, it is alive and well in one form or another. In the way in which English language arts departments and school districts determine booklists, reading lists, and what is deemed acceptable literature, it is very much alive. Altieri (1994) says that canons are "an institutional means of exposing people to a range of idealized attitudes, a range I shall call a *grammar*" (p. 133). Now compare his assertions with those of Giroux:

> Dominant approaches to curriculum and teaching English employ a textual authority as forms of social and political discourse that bear significantly on the ways in which knowledge and classroom social practices are constructed in the interest of relations of domination and oppression. (1994, p. 66).

Figure 3.1

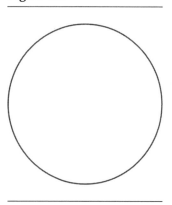

What we see is that in English/Language Arts education, the curriculum often *is* the canon, and therefore expanding one expands the other. I have been very frank in my views about visual literacy in the classroom. I should perhaps sugarcoat my commentary from this point on. Fortuitously, looking at the canon as candy can actually help us along. The canon used to look like Figure 3.1.

The literary canon was for many years like an everlasting gobstopper, or one of those giant jawbreakers one sees in grocery store candy machines. It was pretty much all white and tough to break into. Within its sphere were supposed to be the best of the best writers, so long as they were men and from Western civilizations. Since Matthew Arnold was a strong advocate of the gobstopper canon, Anglos like Shakespeare and Milton seemed particularly qualified.

After a while, though, with the work of women and minority writers gaining in presence and stature and after many other cultural changes, the

Figure 3.2

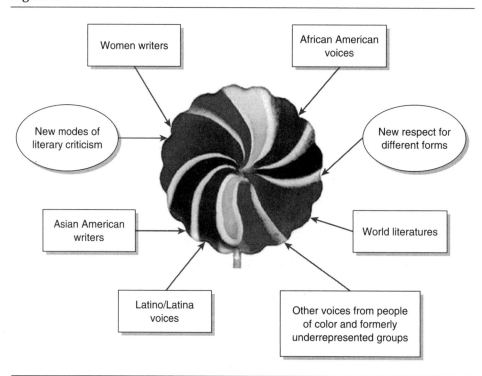

Women writers

African American voices

New modes of literary criticism

New respect for different forms

Asian American writers

World literatures

Latino/Latina voices

Other voices from people of color and formerly underrepresented groups

canon evolved. Rather than being an exclusive sphere encompassing for the most part only white, European males, it became more a plane for multiple voices and experiences, one of those enticingly large, multicolored, swirled lollipops, if you will (see Figure 3.2).

Notice the swirls are in different shades. This new canon is multicultural. Because the canon expanded to include new voices, new opportunities for how to study all literature gained acceptance (or perhaps vise versa) and new forms of writing—and older, less respected forms—gained new appeal. I like to envision the swirls as ever-moving, as centripetal forces drawing in more and more literature and ideas and perspectives. I think it is also worth noting that the canon has reflected our larger culture. In education, notions of canon, curriculum, and culture are tightly intertwined.

We could also see this very text-based canon in terms of what we do with texts: we read them. So, as the canon has expanded, so have notions of reading (see Figure 3.3). What I am asking teachers to do is to continue the progress made in our culture, in our schools, by recognizing the *canon-curriculum-culture connection*. As well, I advocate for teachers to use what the research tells us about imaging, visualization, coding, and reading to extend the arms of the swirls such that they pull in media like comics and graphic novels and continue to expand once-restrictive definitions. Create a "pinwheel lollipop" in your classrooms as you extend notions of literacy, curriculum, and culture to include visual media like sequential-art narratives. Then, share your experiences in journals and conferences to help others build their cases for doing the same.

Figure 3.3

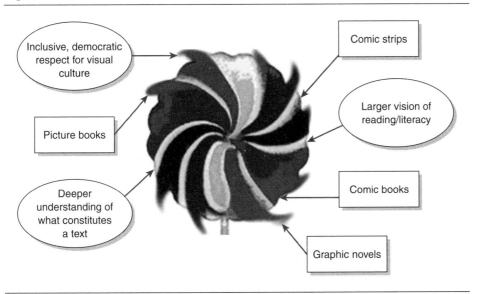

CONCLUSION

There are no easy or simple answers as to why teachers may be reluctant to use comics and graphic novels in their classrooms. The answer may lie in a lack of knowledge of the existing research. It may be due to the graphic novel's relatively recent emergence in the American consciousness. It may be the lack of testimonials from other teachers who have made use of comics and graphic novels. It may be tied into national or local policy issues. It is most likely a convergence of many of these factors and more. However, to examine comics and graphic novels' presence in the classroom as a policy issue at the classroom level is to empower teachers and give them and their students an opportunity for a more democratic, equitable education.

Viewing the situation in terms of the literary canon can provide some insight into why the state of visual media is as it is and can offer hope for how to expand its presence. To confront racism, classism, and elitism is daunting for any teacher, but these have influenced comics, graphic novels, education, culture, and ultimately, curriculum. Even if "dysconscious" in nature, teachers must accept that these elements exist in American schools in one form or another and in our instruction. As I tell a mentor of mine who reminds me to look at opposing viewpoints, "Nobody writes articles about how comics *shouldn't* be used in the classroom," but there are obviously political players in classrooms keeping visual literacy at bay. Indeed, it bears noting that I am not advocating—and no other supporters of visual literacy advocate, to my knowledge—the radical reinvention of the classroom to the point that traditional print texts are thrown out like leftovers. The idea is to augment, to continue to bring in slowly, with the hard work and efforts of dedicated teachers with strong, inclusive notions of democracy and learning who are willing to "be at the vanguard" of policy reform, as DeBlase (2007) has recently called for (p. 119).

Bitter, seemingly impenetrable, traditional notions are winnowing away in favor of sweeter things. It has long been the idea of educators that visual media like comics and graphic novels constituted scurrilous and unnecessary candy, "lollipop culture," if you will, unsuitable for school or life. But as the canon expands, and better understandings of multiculturalism and diversity take hold, we see that it is the canon-curriculum-culture continuum where we need to sink our educational sweet tooth. Only then will we be able to say with confidence that all of our students are being appropriately nourished.

REFERENCES

Altieri, C. (1994). An idea and ideal of literary canon. In D. H. Richter (Ed.), *Falling into theory: Conflicting views on reading literature* (pp. 130–143). Boston: Bedford.

Apple, M. W. (1987). *Teachers and texts: A political economy of class and gender relations in education*. New York: Routledge.

Booth, D., & Gould-Lundy, K. (2006). *"In graphic detail": Using graphic novels in the classroom.* Oakville, Ontario: Rubicon.

Cadiero-Kaplan, K. (2002). Literacy ideologies: Critically engaging the language arts curriculum. *Language Arts, 79*(5), 372–381.

Carter, J. B. (Ed.). (2007). *Building literacy connections with graphic novels page by page, panel by panel.* Urbana, IL: National Council of Teachers of English.

Cary, S. (2004). *Going graphic: Comics at work in the multilingual classroom.* Portsmouth, NH: Heinemann.

Clark, J. M. & Paivio, A. (1991). Dual coding theory and education. *Educational Psychology Review, 3*(3), 149–170.

Deblase, G. (2007). Learning to speak in a political voice. *English Education, 39*(2), 117–119.

Duke, N. K., & Pearson, P. D. (2002). Effective practices for developing reading comprehension. In A. E. Farstrup & S. J. Samuels (Eds.), *What research has to say about reading instruction* (3rd ed., pp. 205–242). Newark, DE: International Reading Association.

Farstrup, A. E., & Samuels, S. J. (Eds.). (2002). *What research has to say about reading instruction* (3rd ed.). Newark, DE: International Reading Association.

Freire, P. (1970). *Pedagogy of the oppressed.* New York: Continuum.

Freire, P. (1973). *Education for critical consciousness.* New York: Continuum.

Gambrell, L. B., & Bales, R. J. (1986). Mental imagery and the comprehension monitoring performance of fourth- and fifth-grade poor readers. *Reading Research Quarterly, 21,* 454–464.

Gardner, H. (1983). *Frames of mind: The theory of multiple intelligences.* New York: Basic Books.

Gardner, H. (1993). *Multiple intelligences: The theory in practice.* New York: Basic Books.

Giroux, H. A. (1994). Reading texts, literacy, and textual authority. In D. H. Richter (Ed.), *Falling into theory: Conflicting views on reading literature* (pp. 63–74). Boston: Bedford.

Gunning, T. G. (2005). *Creating literacy instruction for all students* (5th ed.). Boston: Allyn & Bacon.

Heath, S. B. (1983). *Ways with words: Language, life, and work in communities and classrooms.* Cambridge: Cambridge University Press.

Heer, J., & Worcester, K. (2004). *Arguing comics: Literary masters on a popular medium.* Jackson, MS: UP Mississippi.

King, J. A. (1991). Dysconscious racism: Ideology, identity, and the miseducation of teachers. *Journal of Negro Education, 60*(2), 133–146.

Krashen, S. D. (2004). *The power of reading* (2nd ed.). Portsmouth, NH: Heinemann.

Maria, K. (1990). *Reading comprehension instruction: Issues and strategies.* Parkton, MD: York.

Nieto, S. (2002). *Language, culture, and teaching: Critical perspectives for a new century.* Mahwah: Lawrence Erlbaum Associates.

Ornstein, A. C., & Hunkins, F. P. (2004). *Curriculum: Foundations, principles, and issues* (4th ed.). Boston: Allyn & Bacon.

Paivio, A. (1986). *Mental representations: A dual coding approach.* New York: Oxford University Press.

Postman, N., & Weingartner, C. (1969). *Teaching as a subversive activity.* New York: Dell.

Purcell-Gates, V. (1997). A world without print. In E. Cushman, E. R. Kintgen, B. M. Kroll, & M. Rose (Eds.), *Literacy: A critical sourcebook* (pp. 402–417). Boston: Bedford/St. Martin's.

Sadoski, M., & Paivio, A. (1991). *Imagery and text: A dual coding theory of reading and writing*. Mahwah: Lawrence Erlbaum Associates.

Schnorr, J. A., & Atkinson, R. C. (1969). Repetition versus imagery instructions in the short- and long-term retention of paired associates. *Psychonomic Science, 15*, 183–184.

Smith, M. W., & Wilhelm, J. (2002). *Reading don't fix no Chevys*. Portsmouth, NH: Heinemann.

Spiegelman, A. (1993). *Maus: A survivor's tale*. New York: Pantheon.

Wertham, F. (1954). *Seduction of the innocent*. New York: Rinehart.

Wright, B.W. (2001). *Comic book nation*. Baltimore, MD: Johns Hopkins.

Xu, S. H. (2005). *Trading cards to comic strips: Popular culture texts and literacy learning in grades K–8*. Newark, DE: International Reading Association.

4

Seeing the World Through a Stranger's Eyes

Exploring the Potential of Anime in Literacy Classrooms

Kelly Chandler-Olcott

What is the role of visual literacy in motion? How do students learn from nonwestern forms? Chandler-Olcott explores the history and use of anime, both inside and outside the classroom. She describes the experiences of one adolescent female and provides educators with a primer on the materials and applications of this literary form.

I first met the student I'll call Eileen in 2001 when my research collaborator, English teacher Donna Mahar, convened a focus group of seventh-graders for a project investigating adolescents' technology-enhanced literacy practices. Eileen was one of several students who talked to us that day about using the Internet to explore an interest in Japanese animation, or *anime*, a term that was new to me then. I eventually learned that Eileen's fascination with anime had led her to gather more information about Japan's language and culture and to adopt a variety of discourse practices meant to signal her fandom to others. For example, she employed Japanese, rather than American, emoticons (symbols used to convey emotion) in her e-mails, and she consulted a Japanese-English dictionary from the library to enable her to sprinkle words and phrases such as *kawaii*, which she translated as "cute," throughout her speech and writing. She also expressed pleasure, given what she described as her liberal personal ideology, in the wider range of representations found in Japanese cartoons compared to American ones, explaining to me that she believed "the Japanese have a much better grip on gays, sex, violence, etc. than we do."

The main source of Eileen's passion for anime, however, was her interest in visual art. Talented enough that her drawings were featured in her school's guidance office, she viewed professionally produced anime as a source of inspiration and as a model for improving her own technique. She searched the Internet for images of her favorite characters on which to innovate, created and illustrated her own "fan fictions" (original stories featuring characters from popular media), and ultimately joined an anime-focused electronic mailing list to obtain feedback from others on artwork that she scanned and sent to the group as attachments (see Chandler-Olcott & Mahar, 2001, 2003a, 2003b, for more details on this). For Eileen, the reading and writing activities about which she was most passionate were always connected to her interests in popular culture, and her popular culture fandom was always about producing her own visual texts in response to media, not just consuming the creations of others.

I gained more anime mentors in addition to Eileen when others in my orbit—a computer consultant in the School of Education and an under-graduate advisee—discovered my interest in the topic, often when they saw Eileen's anime-style artwork hanging in my office. After revealing their previously unknown fandom, each recommended helpful Web sites, books, and videos. Simultaneously, I was immersed in scholarship advocating an expanded definition of literacy—one that went beyond traditional print to include a variety of sign systems (e.g., visual, audio, spatial, gestural) that have not traditionally been privileged in school (Eisner, 1991; Gallego & Hollingsworth, 2000; Lapp & Flood, 1995; New London Group, 1996). When I viewed anime fandom from these perspectives, I realized what a powerful example it was of the New London Group's conception of "multiliteracies"—the use of multiple modes of representation to create new meanings, all of them influenced by "the multiplicity of new communications channels and media" and the "increasing salience of cultural and linguistic diversity" in the new global order (Cope & Kalantzis, 2000, p. 5). I resolved to explore anime fandom as a sort of case study—a way to think more concretely about the implications of these new theories of literacy.

This chapter, then, is meant to summarize insights about anime, adolescents, literacy, and pedagogy that I've gleaned over the past five years, with a focus on the potential of this media form to support students' development of visual literacy. The first section provides an introduction to anime as an art form with attention to its history in Japan; its evolution over time; the range of topics it treats; and its reception in the United States, where a fast-growing group of young people are viewing, discussing, and in some cases creating anime of their own. After laying out two different but related arguments for why classroom study of anime can benefit students, I move to the heart of the chapter: a discussion of six instructional approaches that can be used to help students come to deeper and more nuanced understandings of anime specifically and perhaps their popular media interests in general. These activities are supplemented by some recommendations of anime titles and related resources that I see as useful for teachers, many of whom, I'm guessing, will know little more about anime than I did before meeting Eileen.

A BRIEF INTRODUCTION TO ANIME

As Levi (2001) has pointed out, the term "anime" has multicultural origins, even though it refers in a Western context specifically to Japanese animation: "The Japanese took the word from the French to describe all animated films. Then, the Americans took it from the Japanese to describe the unique type of animation that comes from Japan" (p. 1). Although animated films are produced all over the world (Lent, 2001), they have an especially rich tradition in Japan, where they represent about half of all movie ticket sales and are marketed to all age groups, not just children (Napier, 2000). Anime can be found in nearly all genres typically associated in the West with live-action films, including comedy, sports, adventure, romance, crime, and pornography, as well as the science fiction and fantasy genres that have come to be widely associated with the form. Among its common themes are the complexity of romantic relationships and gender identity, the influence of the supernatural, the impact of technology on society, the need for environmental awareness, and the consequences of violence and war (Drazen, 2003).

Given the breadth of topics and genres encompassed by anime, then, a reasonable question to ask might be this: What makes anime recognizable as a media form? From my perspective, two different but related factors are most significant in answering that question: (1) the close kinship between anime and *manga* (Japanese comics and graphic novels), another popular media form in Japan, and (2) a common set of visual characteristics of anime texts that stem partly, though not completely, from those shared origins with manga. Like anime, manga has an enormous commercial and cultural influence in Japan, accounting for nearly 40 percent of the total books and magazines sold (Schodt, 1996) and drawing its audience from people of all ages and social classes. The vast majority of anime series and films were inspired by existing manga, often with minimal adaptation (Napier, 2000).

Visually, the two forms have much in common as well. Both employ narration relying on images more than dialogue to move the story forward (Napier, 2000), and both owe a debt to traditional Japanese art forms. Some scholars point to connections between anime and manga and twelfth-century scrolls from Japanese temples whose impact relied on monochromatic line drawings (Schodt, 1996). Others emphasize similarities to the woodblock prints that flourished in Japan between the sixteenth and nineteenth centuries—images that, like anime and manga, use shading and evocative symbols to create the illusion of more detail than is actually provided for the viewer (Levi, 2001). Anime, which includes multimodal design elements such as audio, gesture, and movement that are absent from manga, also draws on conventions from different kinds of Japanese performance art, including the use of stylized poses to emphasize dramatic moments, borrowed from kabuki theater; and the use of narrative voiceovers accompanying a series of images, borrowed from the *kamishibai* tradition of traveling storytellers who illustrated their narratives on the spot for child audiences (Levi, 2001). Pioneers of Japanese animation such as Dr. Osamu Tezuka were also influenced by techniques used by Walt Disney, most notably his strategies for making characters more expressive by enlarging their eyes (an approach still used by many Japanese directors today). The combination of these influences created a new, hybrid art form—anime—that has been used over time to explore a range of issues and themes but whose essential integrity is still recognizable, especially to Japanese audiences who have grown up with it as a constant presence.

U.S. audiences were introduced to anime in the mid-1960s, when eight Japanese cartoon series were sold in syndication to American television. Although several of these series found modest success, most American viewers did not see them as particularly Japanese because their content and visual features were heavily edited. By 1967, no new Japanese series were being introduced to American viewers, and anime "drew negligible attention outside Japanese ethnic communities" in the United States (Patten, 2001, p. 57). By the late 1970s, however, a number of factors converged to create renewed Western interest in Japanese cartoons, including the rise in popularity in Japan of science fiction cartoons with resemblances to American superhero comics, an increased number of U.S. exchange students in Japan, the availability of the videocassette recorder, and a sanitization of American cartoons when stricter standards for children's television were adopted, making them less appealing to adults (Levi, 2001; Patten, 2001). As more American fans discovered the appeal of imported anime, they organized themselves into fan communities that shared tapes of hard-to-obtain episodes, circulated fan translations of shows that were not already dubbed or subtitled, created original fiction and art using characters and plotlines from favorite shows, and attended conventions, often in costume. The term *otaku*, used derogatorily in Japan to describe hardcore enthusiasts of any popular media form, not just anime, was adopted by American anime fans and largely stripped of its negative connotations (Napier, 2000).

By the early 1990s, anime had begun to penetrate mainstream media in the United States in an unprecedented way. *Sailor Moon*, a fantasy series about the adventures of teenage super-heroines clad in sailor suits, became the first *shojo* (aimed at young girls) anime to be broadcast in the West, with its popularity fueled by the rise of the Internet (Drazen, 2003). The Cartoon Network found success airing *Dragon Ball Z*, a manga-inspired series with a martial arts theme. Then, beginning in the late 1990s, the Pokemon phenomenon swept the country, spawning a plethora of trading cards, stuffed toys, handheld games, and other tie-ins related to the "pocket monsters" that were snapped up by collectors as well as children. While the phenomenon's intensity blazed out quickly, a generation of fans, including Eileen, traces their passion for anime to an interest in Pokemon that expanded when they became aware, often through online explorations, of the range of anime available in Japan.

A number of companies have begun to tap the economic potentials of manga and anime in the United States Several of the major publishing houses, including Del Ray, a division of Random House, and Hyperion, part of the Disney entertainment network, have launched manga lines, and their products are widely available in chain bookstores. American girls, a previously minor market for domestically produced comics and animation, discovered that Japanese media treated a wider range of topics and offered healthier representations of female agency than the U.S. counterparts, and their purchasing power led TOKYOPOP, one of the leading importers of manga and anime to the United States, to implement a series of changes in its marketing meant to attract young females (Jones, 2004). According to an article in *Fortune* magazine (Roth, 2005), this responsiveness to its fan base distinguishes the growing anime/manga industry in the United States from its counterparts in Hollywood or mainstream publishing. By employing the latest technologies to seek fans' input and connecting with fans personally at conventions such as the Anime Expo (attended by 33,000 in 2005), industry leaders, many of whom are self-described *otaku*, have been able to increase both their profits and their audience's satisfaction. This success, in turn, makes it possible for companies to offer an edgier, more diverse range of Japanese offerings to American consumers because they are less concerned with any one title breaking even.

As these trends have converged, more American young people have begun to identify themselves as anime fans. Consequently, literacy teachers can no longer afford to see anime as the province of a few hobbyists seeking to position themselves as "alternative" through their appreciation of

Far Eastern culture. Instead, those who work with young readers and writers need to develop understandings of these fan-related literacy practices that will inform pedagogy and bridge the gap that exists for many students between their out-of-school literacy competence and their in-school achievement (Hinchman, Alvermann, Boyd, Brozo, & Vacca, 2003). While anime films and videos have not, to date, been widely adopted as learning texts in mainstream classrooms, a handful of responsive teachers (Bromley, 2004; Frey & Fisher, 2004; Mahar, 2003) and a growing number of savvy librarians (Halsall, 2004; MacDonald, 2004; Williams, 2003) have experimented with anime in their curricula and their collections, reporting increased participation and engagement when the texts become part of literacy-focused initiatives and projects. These innovators' efforts are squarely in line with the recommendations for reforming English language arts instruction that are discussed in the next section.

How Can Anime Support Students' Acquisition of Visual Literacy Skills?

As I mentioned earlier, one of the most important developments in the field of literacy over the past 15 years or so has been a shift in conceptions of literacy from print-driven reading and writing to "a social, cultural, and contextual phenomenon that exists with relations to many forms of symbolic expression" (Lapp & Flood, 1995, p. 2). For me, the most provocative and elaborate work in this area has been done by a group of scholars calling themselves the New London Group (1996; see also Cope & Kalantzis, 2000). These theorists offered a framework called "multiliteracies" that framed literacy as a design process, one creating meaning through the combination and recombination of available designs—that is to say, the resources, conventions, and sign systems existing for appropriation in the larger culture. According to this view, designs can be expressed in a variety of modes, including, but not limited to, the linguistic, and the most powerful of them—not surprisingly, given the influence of multimedia technologies in our society—are often those that combine more than one mode (e.g., linguistic with visual or visual with audio). To communicate and participate successfully in this world, the New London Group argued, literacy learners need facility with all of these ways of thinking and representing ideas; traditional print literacy skills are not enough.

Arguing that all learners do not develop such facility via existing conceptions of literacy instruction, the New London Group also offered a corresponding pedagogical framework with four components: situated practice (activities grounded in learners' worlds and experience), overt instruction (activities meant to make explicit how designing works), critical framing (activities meant to relate designing to its social contexts and purposes), and transformed practice (the transfer by students of meaning from one context to another). The combination of these approaches was intended to harness the strengths and compensate for the weaknesses of each of them individually—for example, situated practice in concert with overt instruction was meant to tap the motivating aspects of progressive approaches with the efficiency of more direct approaches. As the framers of multiliteracies saw it, this multimodal and multimedia definition of literacy combined with a more powerful and inclusive pedagogy could expand what they called "social futures" (Cope & Kalantzis, 2000, p. 9) for diverse groups of learners.

Lest it appear that these debates about defining literacy have taken place only in small scholarly forums or on the pages of esoteric education journals, let me point out some ways that these shifts in thinking have had a practical impact on K–12 teachers' and students' work. For a decade now, *Standards for English Language Arts*, a document jointly issued by the National Council of Teachers of English and the International Reading Association (1996), has called explicitly for teachers to include "non-print texts" along with print ones and to attend to "visual language" as well as spoken and written language. Repeated references to visual literacy and nonprint media across the twelve standards suggest that the framers saw this expansion of the K–12 curriculum as a comprehensive one—not a superficial add-on. In New York, where I work, the important influence of these recommendations can be seen in the state's performance indicators (see http://www.emsc.nysed.gov/ciai/ela/pub/elals.pdf), which call repeatedly for students at all levels to access, respond to, critique, and create media and electronic texts of various types. The very existence of this edited volume devoted to visual literacy speaks to the power of these trends.

As I see it, anime films and videos can be extremely useful tools for teachers in implementing the vision of the multiliteracies theorists as well as the intent of the NCTE/IRA standards. This is because construction of meaning with anime films and videos as texts requires two levels of proficiency with visual literacy. On the one hand, most anime are remarkably accessible texts for young people because they explore familiar themes and motifs that cut across various cultures; they draw on some predictable visual conventions to develop their narratives; and they supplement their visual messages with other modes such as dialogue, soundtracks, and (often) explanatory liner notes. Consequently, the texts lend themselves easily to instructional approaches that Cope and Kalantzis (2000) have characterized as situated practice: approaches that immerse students in "meaningful practices within a community of learners" (p. 33) and that encourage peer collaboration and risk-taking in heterogeneous settings. As such, anime texts can be good starting points for students unaccustomed to formal instruction in visual literacy.

On the other hand, many aspects of anime texts can be hard for Westerners to understand because, as Levi (2001) has pointed out, they depend on "knowledge of Japan's prehistory, its myths and legends, its religions, artistic traditions, and philosophies" (p. 16). Since the most nuanced and culturally specific information in anime is often carried by images, not dialogue, the form requires and rewards more sophisticated visual literacy skills as well as certain kinds of prior knowledge. Some young people acquire such skills and information outside of school through their membership in various fan communities, both face-to-face and online, but many students do not. Consequently, they "read" anime texts in primarily plot-driven ways, within the narrow frame of reference provided by their Western experiences. This is where sensitively planned classroom instruction around anime texts can nudge students toward more sophisticated meaning-making. Without opportunities for teachers to guide and scaffold students' interactions with these texts, as well as steer them toward relevant and reputable sources of background knowledge about Japanese history and culture (approaches that the New London Group would classify as overt instruction and critical framing), most students are unlikely to achieve these levels of understanding.

That anime can help us internationalize the materials we use in our K–12 curricula (Poitras, 2005) is another powerful reason for including these texts in literacy classrooms. Despite the influence of the multicultural education movement, students in American schools still have too few opportunities to transact with texts originating in countries such as Japan, China, Korea, or Indonesia. If they are assigned Asian texts at all, they tend to be those by authors such as Laurence Yep, Lensey Namioka, or Amy Tan whose works focus mostly on themes such as hybridization or assimilation by first- and second-generation American immigrants. While these perspectives are important to understanding the multiple strands of American culture, they offer students fewer insights into the indigenous customs, history, and language practices of other countries.

Anime texts, in contrast, offer Americans entrée into what Drazen (2003) has called "Japan talking directly to itself" (p. viii) because they are almost exclusively produced for domestic audiences and because they draw on distinctively Japanese history, myths, and traditions. Only very recently did Japanese animators consider that international viewers might be interested in their work, and even then, some of them expressed surprise that anyone outside of Japan would be interested (Levi, 2001). As a result, these films and television series can be examined in terms of their "insider" cultural content, offering students new perspectives on Japan as well as opportunities to think in new ways about American society, media, and values, given the inevitable cross-cultural comparisons. The next section describes a series of instructional approaches designed to maximize these benefits.

RECOMMENDED INSTRUCTIONAL APPROACHES FOR INTEGRATING ANIME INTO LITERACY CLASSROOMS

Keeping in mind that teachers' interest in and comfort level with anime as classroom texts vary, I have organized this section into three parts, each of which describes two different instructional approaches that might be used with anime. Adopting the first two approaches, found in the first part of this section, will likely necessitate the least change in teachers' existing practices, as they do not require the use of particular anime films or episodes in the curriculum but rather invite students to make and reflect on choices of their own. The next two approaches, in the second part of this section, require teachers to select particular anime texts for visual analysis but give them latitude on which texts they use. The final two recommendations, in the last part of this section, are the most prescriptive, as they are tied to an author study of one Japanese director, Hayao Miyazaki, and require more background knowledge about Japanese culture than the others.

Bringing Student-Chosen Anime Into Classroom View

A striking finding of my research has been how little teachers know about students' anime fandom or the literacy practices associated with it, even when students are very committed to their fan-related reading, writing, viewing, and drawing. Sometimes this is true because students wish to keep their interests private; other times, students don't trust their teachers to take those interests seriously. While I respect students' right to share parts of their lives in one context and not another, I am convinced that little stands to be lost and much to be gained if teachers deliberately invite students to share information about their popular-culture preferences. Many English teachers, for example, ask students to complete beginning-of-the-year surveys about their reading and writing habits. It would be easy to include "manga" as one of the list of choices under the heading of "Check everything that you like to read," and yet most teachers do not think to do so. A comprehensive list of film and television genres, including anime, could be included under the heading of "Check everything that you like to watch"—a kind of literacy conspicuously absent, by the way, from most classroom surveys. Teachers could ask students to make suggestions, either anonymous or signed, for popular films and television series that they would recommend to other class members. Each of these moves could contribute to a climate that welcomes young people's interests beyond the sanctioned curriculum. This, in turn, might give some students the confidence to share fan-related expertise that others could draw on, including the teacher. Beyond this information sharing, I see two instructional approaches as promising in terms of bringing students' anime interests into classroom view: film circles and whole-class debriefing of independent viewing.

Film Circles. In the mid-1990s, literature circles—small, student-led groups discussing novels and short fiction—became a widely adopted instructional approach in many language arts classrooms. As Daniels (1994), one advocate of the structure, pointed out, the power of literature circles derives from the way they accommodate student choice, promote collaborative talk, and make students' meaning-making strategies visible to each other. With slight adaptations, "film circles" allow students to explore the wide range of genres and topics treated by anime. The structure is simple but elegant: A group of students with similar interests agrees ahead of time on a film to see together, and then they view it at home, after school, or during study hall, with teachers sometimes convening optional sessions for those students who have difficulty obtaining the films on their own. (See Figure 4.1 for a list of 20 anime titles of interest to middle and high school students that might be a helpful starting point.) To prepare for their group meeting, students take notes with a viewing guide like the one in Figure 4.2 that focuses them on particular visual elements of the film as well as organizes their personal responses. These notes are then used as the starting point for conversation in class, led by a designated discussion leader with assistance from other students playing roles such as timekeeper or recorder. Students are encouraged to bring sketches, not just written notes, to document their ideas for sharing, and they may also (technology permitting) cue up interesting scenes for members to re-watch and discuss.

Figure 4.1   Twenty Anime Titles to Recommend to Students

1. *Akira*	11. *Millennium Actress*
2. *Cardcaptor Sakura*	12. *Mobile Suit Gundam Wing*
3. *Castle in the Sky*	13. *Nausicaa of the Valley of the Wind*
4. *Cowboy Bebop*	14. *Neon Genesis Evangelion*
5. *Dragon Ball Z*	15. *Otaku no Video*
6. *Escaflowne*	16. *Pokemon*
7. *Ghost in the Shell*	17. *Princess Mononoke*
8. *Grave of the Fireflies*	18. *Ranma 1/2*
9. *Kiki's Delivery Service*	19. *Sailor Moon*
10. *Metropolis*	20. *Spirited Away*

Several variations on this structure allow for more student choice regarding titles and might make it easier for students to access those titles for independent viewing, given that they won't all be competing to rent or borrow the same ones. One variant has each student viewing an anime film of his or her choice, then sharing perspectives on it with others who have viewed different texts, focusing their discussion on, for example, the most interesting scene of each film from a visual perspective. In another variant, students work in genre-focused groups, choosing titles within a sub-category of anime such as *mecha*, machine-driven science fiction (e.g., *Mobile Suit Gundam Wing)*, or fantasy (e.g., *Escaflowne*), then discussing how the films compare and contrast with each other in terms of plot/content and animation style. Teachers who employ either approach instead of the more traditional same-text circles will need to allow time for the groups to share brief plot summaries with each other before moving on to visual and thematic analysis, given that students will likely not have seen each other's choices.

Whole-Group Debriefing of Independent Viewing. Another quick, easy way to infuse attention to anime into classroom conversation without formally studying particular texts is to convene a whole-class discussion of students' impressions of the media form after they have viewed their chosen texts. Such a discussion allows learners to pool their knowledge of anime, gleaned across multiple texts, while they air and refine their individual perspectives in light of others' ideas (this can be done as a follow-up to film circles or on its own as a way to process viewing that students do independently). In my experience, these whole-class conversations are enhanced when students write journal entries as a rehearsal for talk, perhaps in response to an open-ended question such as "What visual features of the film you viewed struck you as characteristic of anime?" This will likely yield contributions ranging from "The characters had really big eyes" to "Physical transformation was a big theme of the film, and the animation style made it easy to show that." As students volunteer oral responses, these are recorded for others to consider, either on chart paper or on an overhead transparency. Tallying common features across the group's texts—for example, asking how many students' selections included images of technological transformation or portrayed women in positions of authority—can yield insights about anime in general, not just the individual texts that each student viewed.

Approaches like the two outlined in this section do not depend on teachers' development of a deep knowledge base about anime as a media form or about specific anime titles. What they require is a teacher's willingness to play what Alvermann, Moon, and Hagood (1999) have called the "learner" role relative to his or her students' expertise, as well as a commitment to creating healthy spaces for students to share their insights and ideas with each other. Such openness to out-of-school interests and

Figure 4.2   Sample Viewing Guide for Film Circles

Student Name _____

Date for Film Circle Meeting _____

Film Title _____

Genre _____

Framing	**Lighting/Color**
Jot down any places where you see an interesting close-up or a long shot. Be sure to mention the point in the movie at which it occurs.	Jot down any places where you see an interesting use of color or lighting. Be sure to mention the point in the movie at which it occurs.
Cultural Content	**Personal Response**
Jot down any places where you noticed something about the film (e.g., an image, music, a word or phrase) that struck you as specific to Japanese culture. Be sure to mention the point in the movie at which it occurs.	Jot down what you think about your film overall. What did you like/dislike? What images were most memorable for you and why?

Write any questions that you have about your film that you want to share with your group members:

readiness to share interpretive authority with young people have great potential to reframe classroom communities and position new groups of students as capable, even if they never transact with a common anime text. For these reasons, I see anime-focused film circles and whole-group debriefing of independent viewing as excellent starting points for those practitioners whose curriculum is constrained with a plethora of required texts, those who fear the censorship issues that might be raised by adopting new media in conservative school contexts, or those who want to gauge the degree of students' interest in anime texts before committing instructional time to them. Next, I discuss the pedagogical advantages of teachers and students exploring common texts together, rather than sharing their individual inquiries.

Selecting, Viewing, and Responding to High-Quality Anime Texts

Instructional activities designed to be used with carefully selected, high-quality anime texts are helpful in teachers' attempts to foster more sophisticated visual literacy. As the Multiliteracies framework reminds us, students often lack a shared language for expressing their insights about nonlinguistic texts (Cope & Kalantzis, 2000), and this lack can interfere with their ability to be metacognitive about their viewing. One of the best ways for students to develop that shared language—a key component of critical framing according to multiliteracies pedagogy—is to construct it, with teachers and peers, around a common text. I recognize, however, that selecting this text from the range of anime available will require many teachers to exit their personal comfort zones. So, before I describe the two instructional activities highlighted in this section, let me recommend some resources that may help teachers develop selection criteria for classroom viewing.

Depending on their experience with multimedia in the classroom, teachers may find it helpful to consult a general reference source on teaching film before delving into material focused on anime. While a search of www.amazon.com reveals that dozens of such resources are available, my favorites are those by teachers of young people (see also Chapter 10 by Baines, this volume). For example, *Reel Conversations: Reading Films with Young Adults*, by Alan Teasley and Ann Wilder (1997), includes many note-taking activities to help adolescent viewers attend to literary, dramatic, and—most important for the development of visual literacy skills—cinematic aspects of a film, as well as step-by-step instructions for writing a film review. *Great Films and How to Teach Them* (Costanzo, 2004) is more directed toward the instructor of a film studies class than toward a teacher seeking to integrate film with other literary texts. However, the chapter entitled "The Languages of Film" provides a useful introduction to the semiotics of film, with an emphasis on the idea that the interpretation of visual codes is learned, not natural, behavior. Finally, John Golden's *Reading in the Dark: Using Film as a Tool in the English Classroom* (2001) provides a thorough but accessible introduction to film terminology, as well as offering an excellent chapter connecting viewing strategies to traditional reading strategies such as predicting, questioning, and making personal connections. While none of these books devotes more than a few paragraphs to anime, each offers valuable insights about how films "work" in general.

Fortunately for teachers, anime-specific information can be obtained using the same sources that serve anime's robust fan communities. Early on in our relationship, Eileen introduced me to the Anime Turnpike (www.anipike.com), a clearinghouse site including links to news groups, image galleries, plot synopses, and personal fan pages that remains one of my favorite anime sites today. The best outlet I know for print-based resources is Stone Bridge Press (www.stonebridge.com), a publishing company specializing in material about Japan. Figure 4.3 lists other print and online resources that I see as helpful in locating and selecting high-quality anime.

Figure 4.3   Recommended Anime Resources for Teachers

Print Resources

- *The Animated Movie Guide,* by Jerry Beck (2005): Includes detailed plot summaries about individual titles
- *Anime Explosion! The What, Why, and Wow of Japanese Animation,* by Patrick Drazen (2003): Provides an in-depth discussion of common themes in anime
- "The Anime Revelation," by Jane Halsall (2004): Has a trustworthy list of recommended titles for school libraries
- *Anime From Akira to Princess Mononoke: Experiencing Contemporary Japanese Animation,* by Susan Napier (2000): Especially good on gender issues in anime
- *Watching Anime, Reading Manga: 25 Years of Essays and Reviews,* by Fred Patten (2004): A collection of essays that could be excerpted for student reading
- *Pikachu's Global Adventure: The Rise and Fall of Pokemon,* by Joseph Tobin (2004): Several contributions to this edited collection describe classroom interventions with anime

Online Resources

- *AAU: Index of Anime Reviews* (http://animeworld.com/reviews): A portal to many reviews, alphabetized by title
- *Anime University* (http://www.animeinfo.org/animeu.html): Includes helpful links to course syllabi and research on various aspects of anime
- *The Anime Web Turnpike* (http://www.anipike.com): A very comprehensive fan site
- *Librarian's Guide to Anime and Manga* (www.koyagi.com): A good introductory site, especially on the relationship between manga and anime
- *The Right Stuf International* (http://www.rightstuf.com): Especially good for plot summaries and ratings information on particular titles

My own selection criteria for anime for classroom use include the following:

- Are the themes and issues complex enough to hold the attention of my intended audience?
- Does the text raise themes and issues that can be tied to other required texts, print and/or nonprint, in the curriculum?
- Does the text offer opportunities to explore Japanese culture without alienating or confusing a Western audience?
- Is supplemental material (e.g., director's commentary, storyboards, reviews, etc.) on the text available, either on the DVD itself or on the Internet?
- Is the text visually interesting with high-quality animation?
- If the text includes violence or nudity, are those episodes central enough to the story—and tasteful enough—that I can justify them if called upon to do so?

If I can answer "Yes" to most or all of these questions, then I can be reasonably confident that my anime choice will be appropriate for classroom study, quite possibly using one or both of the two instructional approaches discussed below: mapping visual inferences and film reviews.

Mapping Visual Inferences. Among the most significant contributions of Golden's (2001) book on teaching film in the English classroom is his insistence that many of the skills students use to "decode the visual image are the same skills they use for a written text" (p. xiii). He has called for teachers to use students' interest in and experience with film to help them sharpen skills such as predicting, questioning, and making inferences that can subsequently be applied to more traditional literary texts. What he does not address, however, is that sometimes these skills are more difficult to employ with media texts than they are with print ones. As I noted before, anime films often require viewers to make an inference based on visual information and their prior knowledge and to do so quickly, before the scene cuts to another. For instance, in *Princess Mononoke* (1997), a film by director Hayao Miyazaki (see the next section for more on him), San, a human girl raised by the wolf goddess, is trying to aid the seriously injured Prince Ashitaka by giving him meat to eat. When he is unable to do so, San chews the bits of meat herself to make them tender and transfers them directly from her mouth to his—a tactic I know from personal reading to be used by mother wolves to feed young cubs back at their den. In the film, the scene receives no verbal explanation, but it underscores the hybrid nature of San's existence—a human using wolf behavior to help a human—that serves as a crucial tension of the film. To draw that conclusion, however, requires the viewer to combine real-world knowledge not provided by the text with a small bit of visual information.

A larger-scale example of an anime text whose meaning depends on visual inferences is *Otaku no Video* (1985), based loosely on the experiences of the founders of Gainax Company, Limited, one of the most famous anime studios in Japan. The film intersperses documentary-style, live-action "interviews" of Japanese otaku whose fandom has taken over their lives with animated scenes about two fans who start an anime production studio together. Also included are charts and tables of data from otaku on topics such as how many people who were surveyed admitted to wearing anime costumes to conventions. The juxtaposition of these three different visual representations (live-action film, animated film, and documents) is one of the most important clues that the film is a "mockumentary" or parody—something that the filmmakers never say directly.

To help make such inferences explicit, teachers might model the use of a three-column graphic organizer like the one in Figure 4.4—with the modeling serving, again, as an example of the New London Group's overt instruction. Students can use the form for note-taking during in-class viewing, and then they can gather in small groups to share and discuss their inferences, giving them a chance to practice this skill with less teacher guidance, but with the additional support of peer feedback. Such conversations will help them to realize the degree to which audiences must view "beyond the screen" to understand the message of a film just as they must read "between the lines" to grasp the nuances of a print text. This kind of thinking will prepare them for more formal writing about their anime viewing in the form of a film review, discussed below.

Film Reviews. Experienced teachers of popular media agree that students benefit a great deal from reading and analyzing published film reviews and then writing their own (Costanzo, 2004; Golden, 2001; Teasley & Wilder, 1997). While students can review any film type or genre, anime films offer a wide range of samples for young writers to consult as models because anime are critiqued by both professional film critics doing their jobs and passionate otaku contributing to their fan communities' conversations. Both kinds of reviews are available on the Internet, making it easy for teachers to assemble sets of exemplars for students to compare and contrast.

While many anime films could be used to launch a project on film reviews, *Millennium Actress* (2003) strikes me as a good candidate for secondary students' consideration because of the quality of its animation, the intriguing structure of its tragic love story, and the rich supporting material about its production included on the DVD. The story revolves around Chiyoko Fujiwara, a Japanese actress who starred in films from the 1930s to the 1960s, then abruptly retired to live as a recluse to the present day. When she agrees to be interviewed for a documentary by a filmmaker with a mysterious connection to her past, both he and his cameraman are

Figure 4.4   Sample Note-Taking Guide for Visual Inferences

Film Title: *Princess Mononoke*

Visual Information From Film	Information From My Head	What They Might Mean Together
San chews meat to make it softer and transfers it from her mouth to the mouth of Prince Ashitaka, who is too injured to feed himself	Mother wolves feed their cubs by chewing and regurgitating meat for them back at their dens	San is using aspects of her wolf nature to save a human's life, despite her professed hatred for humans; she's going to be in conflict with herself over this.

literally drawn into the story she tells, appearing as "extras" in her memories about her films and commenting in Shakespearean-like asides on how events are unfolding. From a narrative perspective, these postmodern devices offer students the engaging challenge of distinguishing reality from fiction in light of ambiguous cues (a skill that can easily be transferred to a good deal of classic print literature). From a visual perspective, the interpretive puzzles and temporal shifts are signaled by unusual changes in color and focus.

While the film is a favorite among many anime enthusiasts, online reviews of it are mixed, even contradictory, offering students the opportunity to decide for themselves about the quality of its animation, the believability of its story, and the impact of its flashbacks in time. For this reason, the film is likely to provoke lively discussion and critical thinking regarding how reviewers make and defend their judgments about quality. Figure 4.5 includes a sampling of URL addresses for a variety of opinions about the film authored by both professional reviewers and fans. Other reviews can be found by typing the film title followed by "review" into any popular search engine such as Google.

A review-focused approach to a film like *Millennium Actress* offers teachers the opportunity to employ several components of Multiliteracies pedagogy. After students have viewed and discussed the film over several classes with teacher guidance on an as-needed basis (situated practice), students could be given a packet of reviews of the film or be directed to the relevant bookmarked Web sites to read and compare, perhaps in conversation with a partner. They might then write individual journal entries about which of the reviews came closest to representing their own response to the film (situated practice again). To help them formalize their knowledge and learn to use the language of film critique in context, the teacher could

Figure 4.5   A Sampling of Reviews of *Millennium Actress* (2003)

"Millennium Actress (A New York Times Critic's Pick),*"* by A. O. Scott: *http://movies2 .nytimes.com/gst/movies/movie.html?v_id=259384*

"A Well-Crafted Romantic Drama From the Creators of *Perfect Blue*," by Spence D.: *http://filmforce.ign.com/articles/437/437708p1.html*

"Millennium Actress," by Michael Arnold: *http://www.midnighteye.com/reviews/millactr .shtml*

"Millennium Actress: Truth or Fiction," by Sharon Mizota: *http://www.popmatters.com/ film/reviews/m/millennium-actress.shtml*

"Millennium Actress," by the M-Man: *http://animeworld.com/readerreviews/millennium actress.html*

---

read and annotate a review at the overhead projector, providing a running think-aloud of his or her impressions of the text in terms of its style, structure, and perspective (overt instruction). Next, students could be helped to generate a list of the characteristics, components, and purposes of a film review (critical framing), making explicit and reflecting on what they will need to do in their own writing to produce a successful example of this genre (see Teasley & Wilder, 1997, for a useful rubric to evaluate film reviews). At this point, teachers might ask students, depending on their experience and skill level, to do any number of culminating tasks, including a class-wide review of *Millennium Actress* making direct reference to claims made in the packet of published reviews; group-authored reviews of another anime film viewed in a film circle as described above; or individually authored reviews of a film chosen from the list provided in Figure 4.1. Regardless of how the task is organized, students will have a chance to apply the skills (transformed practice) they learned from the scaffolded activities in which they participated around the core film.

Activities such as mapping visual inferences and writing film reviews allow students to practice literacy skills with high utility for both print and media texts. Since these skills tend not to be intuitive—most students need explicit instruction in order to make mental leaps with texts as well as formulate well-supported arguments in writing—students will benefit from the additional scaffolding provided by teacher modeling and peer discussion around a common text. The genre and topic of those texts can vary tremendously, however, allowing for connections to existing curriculum or students' interests, as the main point of the two activities highlighted in this section is to build transferable skills, rather than cover particular texts. In contrast, I suggest in the next section that teachers consider using a very small cross-section of anime films by a well-regarded director in order to focus more closely on culturally specific aspects as well as to explore in more detail how visual texts such as anime are created.

From Author Study to "Auteur" Study: Spotlighting the Work of Hayao Miyazaki

It's common in print-literacy–dominated English language arts classrooms for students and their teachers to engage in focused studies of a prominent author's work. At the elementary level, such study takes place during teacher read-alouds or in literature circles where groups of children choose a favorite author to explore from a list of teacher recommendations. At the secondary level, students often explore a number of different works by the same author—most notably, William Shakespeare or John Steinbeck—over several years in school. In either case, the practice allows students to make connections between that author's work and their own lives, to consider how one writer treats a theme across different texts, and to use that writer's language choices as a model for their own (Jenkins, 1999).

Teachers interested in promoting visual literacy can use a parallel practice—what I call here "auteur study"—to help students consider how media texts such as anime are constructed. Borrowed from the French word for author, the term "auteur" has come to mean a filmmaker with a distinctive personal style. In anime, the most obvious choice for such study is Hayao Miyazaki, heralded by many as the genre's most luminous figure (Drazen, 2003; McCarthy, 1999). In addition to the critical acclaim his work has received in Japan and around the world (including the first Academy Award for an anime film), the deal struck in 2003 by his Studio Ghibli with Disney–Buena Vista Home Entertainment to distribute his films means that they are more readily available to American teachers than many other anime titles. They have also been dubbed using the voices of Western actors such as Claire Danes and Billy Bob Thornton, making them more accessible to American youth than they would be with subtitles only. Figure 4.6 includes information about five of Miyazaki's films that strike me as having the best potential for classroom use. Biographical information about Miyazaki and critical perspectives about his work can be found in the following:

- *The Anime Art of Hayao Miyazaki* (2006), by Dani Cavallero
- "Flying With Ghibli: The Animation of Hayao Miyazaki and Company" in *Anime Explosion* (2003), by Patrick Drazen
- "Wizard of Light and Shadow" (2003), by Laura Miller (http://www .salon.com/ent/movies/feature/2003/07/10/miyazaki/index_np .html)
- *Hayao Miyazaki: Master of Japanese Animation* (1999), by Helen McCarthy
- The Hayao Miyazaki Web site (http://www.nausicaa.net/miyazaki/ miyazaki)

Figure 4.6   Recommended Miyazaki Films

The following films by Hayao Miyazaki strike me as offering rich opportunities for classroom use. While their Motion Picture Association of America ratings suggest that all five should be generally appropriate for viewing by students in grades 7–12, teachers should view them carefully in light of specific standards for school texts in their communities.

1. *Nausicaa of the Valley of the Winds* (1984)

MPAA Rating: PG

Summary: A thousand years after a global war, a seaside kingdom known as the Valley of the Wind remains one of only a few areas still populated. Led by the courageous Princess Nausicaa, the people of the Valley are engaged in a constant struggle with powerful insects called ohmu, who guard a poisonous jungle spreading across the Earth. Nausicaa and her brave companions, together with the people of the Valley, strive to restore the bond between humanity and the Earth. (*www.rightstuf.com*)

Notes: A rewritten, truncated version of this film was first released in the United States in 1986, sparking controversy among fans. An unedited, redubbed version was made available to the American home-video market in 2005, after the success of *Spirited Away*. The latter version is recommended here.

2. *My Neighbor Totoro* (1988)

MPAA Rating: G

Summary: Satsuki and her little sister Mei move with their father to the Japanese countryside to be near their mother, who is ill in a hospital. Both girls are fascinated by the growing crops and nearby forest, and meet a giant but friendly nature spirit that only innocent children can see. When Mei runs away to visit her mother in the hospital and becomes lost, the Totoro helps Satsuki to find her sister. (Beck, 2005, pp. 176–177)

Notes: This film was named by movie critics Gene Siskel and Roger Ebert as a "Pick of the Year" following its release to American home video in 1994.

3. *Kiki's Delivery Service* (1989)

MPAA Rating: G

Summary: A 13-year-old girl meets the world head on as she spends her first year soloing as an apprentice witch. Kiki is still a little green and plenty headstrong, but also resourceful, imaginative, and determined. With her trusty wisp of a cat Jiji by her side, she's ready to take on the world, or at least the quaintly European seaside village she's chosen as her new home (*www.amazon.com*).

Notes: The English dub of this film features actor Phil Hartman improvising in the role of Jiji the cat in what would be one of his final roles before his death.

4. *Princess Mononoke* (1997)

MPAA Rating: PG-13

Summary: The march of technology, embodied in the dark iron forges of the ambitious Tatara clan, threatens the natural forces explicit in the benevolent Great God of the Forest and the spectral spirits he protects. When Ashitaka, a young warrior from a remote and endangered village clan, kills a ravenous, boar-like monster, he discovers the beast is an infectious demon god, transformed by human anger. Inflicted with its deadly curse, Ashitaka sets out to the forests of the west in search of the cure that will save his life. Once there, he becomes entangled in a bitter battle that matches Lady Eboshi and a proud clan of humans against the forest's animal gods led by the brave Princess Mononoke, who was raised by wolves. (*www.rightstuf.com*)

Notes: This film was the first of Miyazaki's to be dubbed into English with "name" actors from the West such as Claire Danes and Minnie Driver.

5. *Spirited Away* (2001)

MPAA Rating: PG

Summary: Ten-year-old Chihiro and her parents are materialistic Japanese with no interest in their cultural past. They accidentally wander into an old-fashioned community of Japan's supernatural creatures, dominated by a huge bathhouse managed by the witch Yubaba. When Chihiro's parents are turned into pigs, she must work at the bathhouse in order to stay in the fantasy world long enough to save them. (Beck, 2005, p. 266)

Notes: To date, this film is Japan's highest-grossing at the box office of all time. It won the Academy Award for Best Animated Feature Film in 2003.

Just as with print-based author studies, teachers considering an auteur study of Miyazaki will want to expose their students to multiple films by the director, so that the learners can begin to construct inductive understandings of his animation style, his themes, and his characterizations. Students will need to be immersed in his work over a period of time (an approach consistent with situated practice) so that they can see how threads like Miyazaki's commitment to environmental activism cut across films such as *Nausicaa of the Valley of the Winds* (1984), *Princess Mononoke* (1997), and *Spirited Away* (2002). Although it isn't necessary for students to see all of the films featured in an auteur study in their entirety, I would recommend viewing at least two of them from start to finish, given that it may be more difficult for students to understand excerpts from foreign films than it would be for domestic ones. I would encourage students to keep a viewer's log in which they keep notes and sketches from their viewing as well as notes from any background reading they do on the director or particular films. In addition, teachers might want to use large pieces of chart paper that can be posted in the classroom to document contributions to discussion of such questions as "What clues suggest that this is a film by Miyazaki and not some other director?" or "What evidence of the spirit world's influence on daily life do we see in this film?" Two other activities that can be easily combined with a Miyazaki-focused auteur study are mining cultural references and storyboarding, each discussed below.

Mining Cultural References. Miyazaki is known for his extensive knowledge of Japanese history, religion, and myth, and he draws on this knowledge in his films, often in subtle ways. One of the most interesting ways for students to consider what makes his work distinctively Japanese is for them to keep a running list, as they view, of images, music, and historical references that they can follow up through future inquiry, drawing on the many print-based and multimedia texts on Miyazaki, anime, and Japanese history and culture in general.

No matter which Miyazaki films teachers select, there will be myriad cultural references to mine and consider from various viewpoints. In *Princess Mononoke* (1997), for example, Miyazaki makes the story's hero, Prince Ashitaka, a member of the Emishi tribe, a group who lived in the northeast corner of Japan's main island, Honshu, and who fiercely protected their independence from the Japanese emperor until they were defeated by the first Shogun near the end of the eighth century. Students who investigate this group's history will learn that the defeated Emishi lost their culture, eventually becoming assimilated into Japanese society. That Miyazaki chooses to feature an intact Emishi village in a film set more than 600 years after this definitive conflict is an interesting choice to ponder. In the same film, Miyazaki makes the *kodoma*, tree spirits depicted visually as small, ghostlike creatures with large eyes and spinning heads, a central image of rejuvenation for the forest after the deadly battle between two groups of humans is over. My own research into the genesis of the tree spirits, whom I found endearing creatures when I watched *Princess Mononoke* for the first time, revealed that their existence is common in traditional Japanese folktales but that their physical appearance was invented by Miyazaki. This hybrid of tradition and innovation is a hallmark of Miyazaki's work—indeed, of many anime— and provides a terrific example of how the mining of cultural references can lead to students' new respect for the achievements of filmmakers.

To facilitate the cultural mining process, teachers might assign students to groups with a specific focus and then ask them to watch Miyazaki films with that focus in mind. For instance, members of one group might do a little background reading on animism, a traditional Japanese religion that features prominently in Miyazaki's work, in order to be more sensitized to the times when Miyazaki alludes to this tradition. They can then view a film or portions of a film, taking notes about any evidence of animism's influence on the plotline or the images. Students might then follow up their viewing with additional reading online or in print to solve any interpretive puzzles that were raised from watching the film again. The recursiveness of these activities positions viewing as an active pursuit, one that can be informed in powerful ways by reading informational text—an insight that is familiar to anime otaku, although not limited to them.

Storyboarding. One of the most powerful arguments made by the multiliteracies framers (Cope & Kalantzis, 2000; New London Group, 1996) and others in their calls for expanded conceptualizations of literacy is for students to engage in visual media production, not just response and critique. Assignments like cultural-reference mining and film reviews encourage students to engage with visually oriented texts such as anime, using "sets of lenses" distinct from those that they might employ with traditional print. However, such assignments do tend to have the drawback of positioning students as anime consumers rather than potential anime creators. While it's unlikely that many middle or high school students will have available to them the sophisticated resources and technologies necessary to do full-scale animation of their own, some techniques exist that can help them explore the ways of thinking and representing ideas that an animator typically uses. The storyboard, described by Teasley and Wilder (1997) as "a series of drawn frames, one frame per shot, with a description of the action or dialogue written underneath the frame" (p. 69), is a visual tool that can be helpful in showing students how anime texts are created and conceptualized.

A study of Miyazaki's work can be an excellent context in which to consider storyboarding because so much background information is available about this director's creative process. The DVD of *Spirited Away*, for example, includes many examples of his storyboards, including a series of sketches for the film's opening scenes that reveal, perhaps more powerfully even than the finished product itself, how he hoped to convey the initial petulance and self-centeredness of his heroine, Chihiro, through her posture in the back seat of her parents' car. In addition, VIZ Media, an anime-focused company, has published impressively illustrated print texts to accompany many of Miyazaki's films. Their *Spirited Away* companion includes storyboards just as the disc does, but it also includes interviews with Miyazaki, as well as with his supervising animator and his art director. Each man provides different insights about the film's visual elements, ranging from the use of red as a signature color to unify the exterior shots to the reconceptualization of the dragon character's face as more dog-like to make him less "cold and mysterious" (Miyazaki, 2002, p. 148).

Supplemental materials like these offer teachers (including those who don't see themselves as talented visual artists) unprecedented opportunities to model and open up for student discussion a range of strategies related to the production of visual texts. After viewing several of Miyazaki's films and learning about the process by which they were created, students will be much better prepared to devise their own storyboards, whether they're in an anime style or not, for texts that they choose or are assigned. They will have the opportunity to develop the understanding that media texts don't just "happen"—rather, they are constructed carefully by collaborative teams who constantly rethink their own work. At this point, students might profitably be assigned a task developed by Golden (2001): the storyboarding, often in small groups, of the first ten shots or so of a particular literary text (see Figure 4.7 for the chart that Golden gives his students to organize their thinking). Having had access to model storyboards from a master filmmaker like Miyazaki can only enhance students' efforts in such an activity. While students can use stick figures and symbols to sketch their ideas for these storyboards, those with an interest in anime-style art may want to be more elaborate with the visual portions of the chart, possibly with tips from a reference like Christopher Hart's *Anime Mania: How to Draw Characters for Japanese Animation* (2002). Others might want to use computer software programs such as iMovie or PowerPoint if they are available.

Storyboarding and cultural reference mining can help students to access information from both print and electronic sources to enrich their anime viewing, as well as their own creation of print and visual texts in response to that viewing. By focusing on a director such as Miyazaki, about whom much has been written, teachers ensure that their students will have a wealth of data to sort through and select from—key skills to develop in an age of information overload. At the same time, a focus on Miyazaki, whose work is firmly grounded in Japanese myth, religion, and history, increases the chances that they will engage in true cross-cultural analysis. Miyazaki himself has written about the benefits of such culturally relevant texts for the Japanese:

> Surrounded by high technology and its flimsy devices, children are more and more losing their roots. We must inform them of the richness of our traditions. I think the world of film can have a striking influence by fulfilling the traditional functions, as a piece of a vividly colored mosaic, to a story which can be applied today. That means, at the same time, we can gain a new understanding of what it means to be residents of this island country. (Miyazaki, 2002, p. 16)

It isn't difficult to imagine that Miyazaki's stories can fulfill similar functions for those who do not reside in his "island country" but who are linked to that nation via trade, diplomacy, and popular media.

Figure 4.7 Storyboarding Activity From Golden (2001)

Title of Text:

Pages:

Summary of Scene:

Shot #1

(sketch goes here)	Intended effect of shot: Diegetic sound (heard by characters): Nondiegetic sound (heard only by audience):

Lighting:

Shot type:

Angle:

Movement:

Edit:

SOURCE: Adapted from Golden, J. *Reading in the dark: Using film as a tool in the English classroom.* Copyright 2001 by the National Council of Teachers of English.

CONCLUDING THOUGHTS

My five-year inquiry into anime has shown me how passionate and thoughtful anime enthusiasts are about their fandom. With few exceptions, they share carefully considered reasons for why they like certain animators' styles, why they construct particular interpretations of favorite images, and why they depict their own anime-influenced original characters in particular ways to create desired effects. Their articulateness about such matters is in stark contrast to the kinds of responses I received from all but the most avid readers of print-based fiction when, while teaching secondary English, I asked them about their literary preferences. (It's similarly interesting to note that those readers, unlike anime fans, tended to position themselves as consumers of stories but rarely as producers of them.) I raise this point not to suggest that anime films are more valuable than traditional literature or that anime fans are more sophisticated than readers of books—if there's anything I've learned from taking young people's popular culture interests seriously as a researcher, it's that such hierarchies are almost always unproductive, no matter which texts are elevated in them. Instead, I hope to demonstrate that anime texts have a good deal to teach viewers about various meaning-making strategies that can be applied to a host of other forms as well. Furthermore, I hope to show that anime fan communities have ways of apprenticing their members into sophisticated viewing practices that could, with a bit of adaptation, be adopted in classroom literacy contexts, making instruction more engaging and effective for a wide range of learners.

In arguing, as I have done here, that classroom study of anime texts can play a role in supporting young people's development of visual literacy, I do not mean to suggest that this role will necessarily be a large one, or that it will happen in every class with a literacy focus. There are plenty of other forms of popular culture—graffiti art, step dancing, computer gaming, just to name a few—that have been embraced by young people while remaining marginalized in formal academic settings. Any number of these pursuits might be more appropriate choices for opening up the curriculum and expanding definitions of literacy in a given classroom than anime. That said, my experiences with anime fans, as well as my reading of the small but provocative body of research on anime and manga (Chandler-Olcott, in press), mean that the following argument by anime scholar Antonia Levi (2001) resonates for me:

> American otaku often say that anime's charm lies in its unpredictability, its off-beat weirdness that makes you stop and think about things you never even noticed before. In fact, anime is more creative for Americans than it is for Japanese. It's a chance to see the world through a stranger's eyes, and that's a view that ensures we'll never look at ourselves quite the same way again. (p. 17)

Students who explore anime in a more formal way aren't the only ones who are likely to look at their worlds and themselves in a new way. Ultimately, what a given class learns about anime from a literacy teacher experimenting with the methods I've advocated here may be less important than what that teacher stands to learn from an anime-focused inquiry about young people and their position in a world that is becoming more globalized and interconnected in some ways and, almost paradoxically, more fragmented into interest groups in other ways (Cope & Kalantzis, 2000). Anime fandom reflects that process in a microcosm. Taking it seriously can help all of us who care about reading, writing, and viewing in these complex times as means for generating new insights and developing new classroom practices. While I am certain that no chapter on anime, however comprehensive, can substitute for the committed mentorship of an ardent young fan, I hope that this one will encourage other teachers to explore this fascinating media form on their own, perhaps by identifying and collaborating with students whose fandom, like Eileen's, remains untapped in their classrooms today.

REFERENCES

Alvermann, D., Moon, J. S., & Hagood, M. (1999). *Popular culture in the classroom: Teaching and researching critical media literacy*. Newark, DE: International Reading Association.

Beck, J. (2005). *The animated movie guide*. Chicago: A Cappella Books.

Bromley, H. (2004). Localizing Pokemon through narrative play. In J. Tobin (Ed.), *Pikachu's global adventure: The rise and fall of Pokemon* (pp. 211–225). Durham, NC: Duke University Press.

Cavallero, D. (2006). *The anime art of Hayao Miyazaki*. Jefferson, NC: McFarland & Company.

Chandler-Olcott, K., & Mahar, D. (2001). Considering genre in the digital literacy classroom. *Reading Online, 5*(4). Retrieved December 2, 2004, from http://www.readingonline.org/electronic/elec_index.asp?HREF=/ electronic/chandler/index.html

Chandler-Olcott, K., & Mahar, D. (2003a). Adolescents' anime-inspired fanfictions: An exploration of Multiliteracies. *Journal of Adolescent and Adult Literacy, 46*, 556–566.

Chandler-Olcott, K., & Mahar, D. (2003b). Tech-savviness meets Multiliteracies: An exploration of adolescent girls' technology-mediated literacy practices. *Reading Research Quarterly, 38*, 356–385.

Chandler-Olcott, K. (in press). Anime and manga fandom: Young people's Multiliteracies made visible. In J. Flood, D. Lapp, & S. B. Heath (Eds.), *Handbook of research on teaching literacy through the communicative, visual and performing arts*. Mahwah, NJ: Lawrence Erlbaum.

Cope, B., & Kalantzis, M. (2000). *Multiliteracies: Literacy learning and the design of social futures*. New York: Routledge.

Costanzo, W. (2004). *Great films and how to teach them*. Urbana, IL: National Council of Teachers of English.

Daniels, H. (1994). *Literature circles: Voice and choice in the student-centered classroom.* York, ME: Stenhouse.

Drazen, P. (2003). *Anime explosion! The what, why, and wow of Japanese animation.* Berkeley, CA: Stone Bridge Press.

Eisner, E. (1991). Rethinking literacy. *Educational Horizons, 69,* 120–128.

Frey, N., & Fisher, D. (2004). Using graphic novels, anime, and the Internet in an urban high school. *English Journal, 93*(3), 19–26.

Gallego, M., & Hollingsworth, S. (2000). *What counts as literacy: Challenging the school standard.* New York: Teachers College Press.

Golden, J. (2001). *Reading in the dark: Using film as a tool in the English classroom.* Urbana, IL: National Council of Teachers of English.

Halsall, J. (2004). The anime revelation. *School Library Journal, 50*(8), 6–12.

Hinchman, K., Alvermann, D., Boyd, F., Brozo, W., & Vacca, R. (2003). Supporting older students' in- and out-of-school literacies. *Journal of Adolescent & Adult Literacy, 47,* 304–310.

Jenkins, C. B. (1999). *The allure of authors: Author study in the elementary classroom.* Portsmouth, NH: Heinemann.

Jones, V. (2004, July 28). Girl power: Young women are driving one of the hottest trends in pop culture. *Boston Globe.* Retrieved September 8, 2004, from ProQuest database.

Lapp, J., & Flood, D. (1995). Broadening the lens: Toward an expanded conceptualization of literacy. In K. A. Hinchman, D. J. Leu, & C. K. Kinzer (Eds.), *Perspectives on literacy research and practice* (pp. 1–16). Chicago, IL: National Reading Conference.

Lent, J. (2001). *Animation in Asia and the Pacific.* Bloomington, IN: Indiana University Press.

Levi, A. (2001). New myths for the millennium: Japanese animation. In J. Lent (Ed.), *Animation in Asia and the Pacific* (pp. 33–50). Bloomington, ID: Indiana University Press.

MacDonald, H. (2004). Drawing a crowd: Graphic novel events are great ways to generate excitement. *School Library Journal, 50*(8), 20–22.

Mahar, D. (2003). Bringing the outside in: One teacher's ride on the anime highway. *Language Arts, 81*(2), 110–117.

McCarthy, H. (1999). *Hayao Miyazaki: Master of Japanese animation.* Berkeley, CA: Stone Bridge Press.

Miyazaki, H. (2002). *The art of Miyazaki's Spirited Away.* San Francisco: VIZ Media.

Napier, S. (2000). *Anime from Akira to Princess Mononoke: Experiencing contemporary Japanese animation.* New York: Palgrave.

New London Group. (1996). A pedagogy of multiliteracies: Designing social futures. *Harvard Educational Review, 66*(1), 60–92.

Patten, F. (2001). Anime in the United States. In J. Lent (Ed.), *Animation in Asia and the Pacific* (pp. 55–72). Bloomington, ID: Indiana University Press.

Patten, F. (2004). *Watching anime, reading manga: 25 years of essays and reviews.* Berkeley, CA: Stone Bridge Press.

Poitras, G. (2005). The teacher's companion to *The Anime Companion.* Retrieved December 27, 2005, from http://www.koyagi.com/teachers.html

Roth, D. (2005). Anime explosion! It's profitmon! *Fortune.* Retrieved November 30, 2005, from http://www.fortune.com/fortune/investing/articles/0,15114,1134596-2,00.html

Schodt, F. (1996). *Dreamland Japan: Writings on modern manga*. Berkeley, CA: Stone Bridge Press.

Teasley, A., & Wilder, A. (1997). *Reel conversations: Reading films with young adults*. Portsmouth, NH: Heinemann/Boynton-Cook.

Tobin, J. (2004). *Pikachu's global adventure: The rise and fall of Pokemon*. Durham, NC: Duke University Press.

Williams, L. P. (2003, October 9). Library film fest aimed at teenagers; Japanese animation hopes to reel 'em in. *Times-Picayune*. Retrieved September 21, 2004, from ProQuest database.

5

"Literary Literacy" and the Role of the Comic Book

Or, "You Teach a Class on What?"

Rocco Versaci

Can reading and discussing comic books constitute literate behavior? It depends on what you do with them. In this chapter, Versaci provides a history of comics and their fall from favor and describes how he uses them in his classes. His insights into the visual and literary features found in comic books will ensure that you never look at them again in quite the same way.

One of my most discouraging moments as a teacher came pretty early in my career. During one of my composition classes, I planned to have a discussion with my students about what creative works they connected with and why. In preparation for this discussion, I asked them to list their favorite book, movie, television show, and CD or song. Then I asked them to consider how these various works spoke to who they were—what was it about these particular stories, characters, sights, and sounds that they found so attractive? Why did they return to these particular creative works over and over again?

The students in that class were bright and engaged, so I looked forward to a fun and thought-provoking discussion. As they worked, I strode up and down the aisles to peek at their lists. What I saw on my first pass, however, gave me pause. On list after list, students had left the "favorite books" part blank and were working instead on the other categories. I kept checking, hoping that this was an anomaly of the first row, but no, the vast majority of my students had empty spaces instead of book titles. Ever hopeful, I asked if people were having trouble picking a favorite book because there were so many memorable ones to choose from, and they were stymied because it was too hard to pick just one.

They weren't. As one student put it, "I don't really read books." This sentiment was quickly echoed by his peers.

The many other classes that I have taught since then and in which I asked my students to do the same thing have yielded similar results. Based on these and other classroom experiences, on conversations that I have had with colleagues, and on the mountains of research addressing various crises of student reading habits, the sad conclusion that I have drawn is that to the vast majority of our students, books simply don't matter.

How can this be? For me, books were always important. On summer days back in the 1970s, when I was an adolescent growing up in the Chicago suburbs, my favorite place to be was a stifling little room upstairs in my parents' house, curled up with a book on an itchy couch that magnified the wet Midwestern heat. Who needed the great outdoors when there were so many other worlds to explore—Oceania; Watership Down; Francie Nolan's neighborhood in Williamsburg, Brooklyn, during the summer of 1912? To me, these were real places, and those who inhabited them were real people (or, in the case of *Watership Down*, rabbits). Later, in high school, reading literary works like *King Lear, The Stranger,* and *Catcher in the Rye* was a revelatory experience. These stories had ideas. They raised issues. They made me think about my own life, the people in it, the myriad experiences yet to be lived, and the many difficult choices yet to be made. In short, I loved to read.

Loving to read is more than simply knowing how to read. The issue—and problem—for many of our students is one of literacy, but a great deal depends on not defining that word too narrowly by reducing it to mean only the ability to read and write. That "literacy" refers to much more than word mastery has been a topic of debate for many years now, beginning with Friere and Macedo's notion that the true power of literacy is political, whereby readers will, ideally, "read the world and the word" (Greco, 1992, p. 83). Their ideas have been a touchstone for the many education scholars who have continued to define and redefine "literacy" as something beyond obtaining a neutral set of skills and toward using those skills to create real-world results. Cadiero-Kaplan (2002) has outlined a hierarchy of "literacies" based upon the degree of empowerment they offer to the reader/student. The highest level in this hierarchy is "critical literacy," whereby students "engage texts and discourses inside and outside the classroom" (p. 377), and become people who "actively participate in a democracy" (p. 378).

That such action can be tied to the act of reading a book is an assumption shared by these educators, and the reality of that assumption is articulated, perhaps most directly, by Peter Whittaker (2001) in his essay, "What's the Point of Fiction in a World Full of Trouble?" It does not take him long to answer his own question:

> reading is one of the most radical things you can do. It is no surprise that autocrats, from the destroyers of the Library at Alexandria to the Nazis and the Taliban, make a habit of burning books. Books give us access to knowledge, opinion, and debate. They open up all the possibilities that those who wish to control and oppress would deny us. (p. 9)

Making Whittaker's views even more concrete is the work of Jun-Chae Yoon (2001), who in his essay "Literacy Practices in Dark Times: A Reflective Memoir," has described the important role that reading played for him and other students while growing up in the oppressive regime of South Korea during the 1980s. In this memoir, Yoon describes joining an underground reading group whose members had to read "handwritten transcriptions" (p. 291) of books because of the danger of discovery. It was during the course of participating in this group—and as a direct result of their covert reading and discussion—that Yoon asked himself, "Was I to be an activist or a bystander?" (p. 292). He chose the former.

What these and other thinkers suggest is that true literacy requires the reader to engage much more with the act of reading than simply recognizing words on a page; in the case of the above examples, this engagement is political. While I certainly value political activism, my immediate goal as a teacher of writing and literature is somewhat different. Put bluntly, my goal is to correct the problem that too many students will not become lifelong readers—people who love to read because they understand the attendant joys that reading brings: losing oneself in another world, grappling with important ideas that become animated through narrative, gaining greater appreciation for those from diverse backgrounds, developing appreciation for a well-crafted artistic statement, desiring to tell stories of one's own. For those of our students who regard books either suspiciously or with dread, the literature handed to them by people like me in English classes across the country almost immediately becomes a task to be endured rather than texts to be explored, remembered, and emulated.

By itself, the word "literacy" does not capture the promise of lifelong reading; what is needed, I believe, is a term that is more focused to suggest this passion for books: "literary literacy." An iteration of this term comes from Perloff (1997), in an editorial that appeared in the *Chronicle of Higher Education*. In this piece, Perloff argued that the profession of literary studies has become too specialized, too insular, too focused on teaching a form of reading based on "cultural unmasking" (p. B4). She contended that teachers of literature need to concentrate more on making literary study "valid" to students (and, thus, to those who fund education), and doing so means making students more aware of the relationship between literature and life (p. B5). Perloff's motivation was largely pragmatic, offering suggestions for how literary programs in higher education can claim a bigger piece of an ever-dwindling pie. Obtaining such funding is of course important, but my version of "literary literacy" is informed by the idea that a love of reading is an end in itself; after all, a life without stories is a much poorer life. This issue of helping our students become lifelong readers is one faced by all English and language arts teachers at all levels of education, and my suggestions in the pages that follow can be adapted and enacted by educators from kindergarten onward. All of my suggestions stem from my belief that to foster literary literacy, we must present students with engaging reading material that rewards meaningful analysis, demonstrates important connections with their lives, and invites them to take an active role in their literary education rather than be passive consumers of it.

And here's the kicker: one of the best kinds of "engaging reading material" that achieves these goals is the comic book.

The irony is all too apparent. For most of their history, despite—or perhaps because of—periods of popularity, comic books have been denigrated as sub-literate trash. In the 1940s, also known as the "Golden Age" of comics, this medium enjoyed a popularity that has never been equaled; by mid-decade, 90 percent of kids aged eight to fifteen were regular comic book readers (Benton, 1993). The size and age of this readership prompted sharp criticism, sparking a national debate that led one critic to conclude that comics were a "poison" whose antidote lay in bookstores and libraries and that any "parent who [did] not acquire that antidote [was] guilty of criminal negligence" (as cited in Nyberg, 1998, p. 4). Predictably, the main charges were that comics negatively impacted student literacy, that "comic-book readers [were] handicapped in vocabulary building because in comics all the emphasis is on the visual image and not on the proper word" (as cited in Giddins, 2004). Despite several studies that determined that "reading comic books, even to the exclusion of other activities, seemed to make little difference in reading skills, academic achievement, or social adjustment" (Nyberg, 1998, p. 11), the comic book retained its reputation as something that could cause only harm to young readers.

This "harm" took on a decidedly sociological cast in the 1950s, when comic books were cited as a prime cause of juvenile delinquency (Nyberg, 1998, p. 18). One of the main forces behind this accusation was Dr. Fredric Wertham, who in 1953 published his anti-comic crusade *Seduction of the Innocent*—a "study" based largely on anecdotal evidence and questionable logic. His conclusion, in essence, was that comic books caused delinquency because he interviewed several imprisoned juvenile delinquents who told him that they read comics (Sabin, 1993). The very next year, 1954, saw the beginning of the "Kefauver Hearings," which were nationally televised Senate hearings designed to investigate the issue of comics' negative effects on children. One of the witnesses was Wertham himself, who in typical overstated fashion declared that "Hitler was a beginner compared to the comic book industry" (as cited in Sabin, 1993, p. 159). These hearings, fueled by negative public sentiment, led publishers to create the Comics Code Authority, whose sole mission was to enforce the "Comics Code," widely regarded as the most restrictive ratings code that any entertainment medium in this country has faced (Benton, 1993, p. 53).[1] In order for a title to receive the "Seal of Approval," it had to conform to the strictures of the Code, which meant, in part, that it had to avoid complex characterization— especially as regarded "official" figures like police officers and judges—and topics that might be of interest to older readers (Sabin, 1993). The end result of the Code and the publishers' conformity was the mainstream "juve- nilization" of the medium, which in turn caused the general public to view comic books as a form suitable only for children.

This misapprehension persists today. And yet, comic book artist and writer Scott McCloud (1994) has warned that we should not judge an entire medium based simply upon its most popular manifestations. When I discuss with my students the common perception that comic books are an inferior art form to books or film, I remind them of a pithy bit of wisdom espoused by science fiction writer Theodore Sturgeon: "Ninety percent of anything is crud" ("Sturgeon's Law"). Just like comics, books and film have their crud. Unlike comics, however, no one dismisses the latter two forms because of this crud. After all, how foolish would it be to disparage the entire medium of film outright simply because one did not find big budget Hollywood movies to be either interesting or artistically redeeming? Yet this position, which seems ludicrous as stated above, is exactly the kind of thinking that most people engage in when considering comic books.[2] But as McCloud and others well know, the form itself is remarkably complex, "provid[ing] wide opportunities for detailed exposi- tion, complex visual/verbal effects, pacing in time and space, and . . . artis- tic control of how a reader perceives a narrative structure" (Witek, 1989, p. 9). This complexity emerges due to the blending of both words and pictures;

the combination of those two representational devices creates a unique kind of "graphic language," where meaning "does not 'happen' in the words, or the pictures, but somewhere in-between, in what is sometimes known as 'the marriage of text and image'" (Sabin, 1993, p. 9).

This marriage is particularly relevant to the subject at hand because for our students, literacy does not simply involve the written word. One possible reason our students no longer read is that their lives are filled with so much other information to process: film, television, the Internet. What these media share, of course, is a visual component that, sadly, is often passively received. If part of our job as English teachers is to make our students life-long readers who are astute and eager interpreters of the world around them—and I believe it is—then we need to address our students' visual literacy. Simply put, visual literacy "is to images what reading and writing are to words[; . . . it] relates to a person's ability to interpret and create visual information—to understand images of all kinds and use them to communicate more effectively" (Simons, 2002, p. i). The importance of students' developing visual literacy cannot be overstated, for "visual literacy is a requirement for clear thinking in the 21st century" (Hoffmann, 2000, p. 220). The problem, however, is that the study of visual images takes on increasingly less importance as students progress through their education (Bustle, 2004), and their study, too often, becomes the exclusive province of students studying art or photography (Hoffmann, 2000; Oring, 2000).

TEACHING VISUAL LITERACY WITH COMICS

Comic books—more so than any other visual medium—allow teachers to pose questions that help students do two things: understand how images produce meaning, and become engaged in the search for this meaning. Unlike film and television, which unspool at a predetermined rate and are experienced more or less passively, comics can be read at whatever pace the reader desires. And "read" is a key word here. As Roger Sabin argues, "reading a comic . . . takes an amazing number of eye movements to understand a panel—flicking from picture to text and back again" (1993, p. 6). In fact, a great number of eye movements are necessary simply to apprehend the narrative content of a panel; certainly more are necessary to interpret deeper meaning. The point here is that any given comic book panel contains a variety of information that must be processed, and the "static" format allows a teacher to spend time focusing on analytical skills like those needed to study a still photograph.

But unlike photography, comics are largely driven by narrative, so one "picture" signifies not only by itself but also in relation to the other "pictures" that surround it. When reading an entire page of comics—especially one put together by a skilled visual architect—the reader's eye is very active and not always working in the simple left-to-right motion that reading requires. In many ways, the act of reading a comic cuts much more closely to how our students today receive information. I'm thinking particularly of the Internet, where the sites that I see my students visiting regularly are densely packed and ask readers to move their eyes diagonally and up and down in addition to side to side—the same kind of movements that come with reading comic book panels and pages. Thus, visually speaking, comics lend themselves to extensive interpretation, providing teachers with numerous opportunities to help develop visual literacy among their students. Teachers may pose to their students several interesting analytical questions. "How would you describe the style of these pictures?" "How does this drawing style interact with the story?" "Why these particular pictures?" "Why in this particular arrangement?" "How would different visual elements change the story?" The answers to these questions and other related questions are not obvious, but because comic books reward this kind of meaningful analysis, students begin to see themselves as knowing how to assemble and uncover the deeper meaning of a work.

In order to help my students see themselves as critics, I have developed several comics-related assignments that highlight connections between visual information and thematic subtext. Because visuals can be complicated or overwhelming, teaching visual literacy is a tricky operation, and teachers should move students through a series of assignments that become more and more challenging. My "foundation" in this approach is an assignment that I call "panel analysis," which students can do in a short paper or as an individual or group in-class activity. The assignment asks the student to choose a single panel from a comic book and to analyze that panel. To do this, they must perform two main tasks. First, they must describe the visual and textual elements within the panel, and second, they must interpret possible deeper meaning in those elements. We spend time in class discussing how images signify: composition (the arrangement of materials within a space), viewing angles and distance, shading (including use of color), use of text, style of drawing, size and shape of panel, and type of border. Students, using our discussion as background, apply the ideas to their chosen panel in order to uncover how the panel "works" in terms of both narrative and theme. Teachers can conduct this exercise with any comic book panel where the details are rich enough to suggest meaning that is not readily apparent—in other words, a panel that will reward close analysis. When I give this assignment to my students, I use James Sturm's graphic novel *The Golem's Mighty Swing* (2001), a beautifully drawn and written story about the Stars of David, a traveling Jewish baseball team in the 1920s. Sturm's drawing style is understated and deceptively simple; in truth, he's a master of design, and he dispatches the various elements of visual style to evoke unspoken meaning. In my class, students are responsible for choosing their own panel to analyze, and this element of choice helps them to see themselves as active, interpretive readers, where an important first step is judging the "interpretability" of an image or set of images.

To help them with their choice, I always provide a model in our class discussion, and one panel that I have used from Sturm's book depicts Mo, sixteen-year-old brother of the book's narrator, sulking around town after a victory on the road (see Figure 5.1). Like the majority of panels in Sturm's book, this one is very evocative and lends itself to highlighting the different ways that an image signifies. Specifically, we discuss the viewing angle and distance—and in particular how Sturm's use of a high-angle long shot for his perspective makes Mo look small and insignificant, a reflection of his inner conflict of not quite knowing whether he's good enough to get what he wants (to play second base for the Brooklyn Dodgers). Also, Sturm composes the frame so that Mo walks from right to left and from bottom to top. This direction is the exact opposite in which an eye moves across a panel, so the effect is somewhat jarring, causing the reader's eye to slow down and emphasizing the "difficulty" of Mo's outward and inward journey. This subtle struggle is underlined by the accompanying text—his brother's comments to another player, Wire, in a different scene. Also suggesting this struggle is Sturm's shading, which captures the somberness of late afternoon.

All of our discussion, which eventually becomes exhaustive, serves as a model for the students in their own investigation of a panel. The results of this assignment are typically gratifying; when confined to a panel-sized space, students are able to focus their attention and powers of interpretation. As a result, they read the images at an impressively deep level and are able to connect "local" meanings within the panel to "global" themes throughout the book. When I conduct this activity in small groups, with several pairs of eyes at work on a single panel, the results are even more startling. Overall, the exercise is a very engaging and useful way to help students develop their visual literacy, where not only do they notice different significant visual features, but they interpret them in order to identify how these features attempt to influence a viewer or reader, and they begin to feel confidence in their interpretations.

The analysis of a single panel forms the basis for more complicated tasks that will continue to empower students as readers who enjoy searching for meaning in what they read. My next assignment focuses on layout, or the arrangement of panels on a page or over the course of several pages. This feature is a key component of comics' graphic language, and, given that layout multiplies the visual and textual information, its analysis requires a more sophisticated set of interpretive skills. My favorite exercise involves a puzzle. Specifically, I focus on a page from an extraordinary story by Jaime Hernandez (1991) titled "Flies on the Ceiling" (see Figure 5.2). Hernandez's work is influenced by the magic realism of authors like Carlos Fuentes and Gabriel García Márquez, and in "Flies," the main character, Isabel, travels to Mexico in an effort to escape the guilt she feels over various "failings" in her life. While there, however, she encounters many fantastical occurrences that thwart this effort. On this particular page, Isabel encounters a strange black-clad man who may or may not be real: Is he a figment of her tortured conscience, or is he an incarnation of the Devil

Figure 5.1

himself? Hernandez lays out this brief encounter in a standard nine-panel grid where each panel is of uniform size and shape. A careful examination of the entire page reveals Hernandez's deft use of silence (i.e., no text), shifting visual perspectives, and the visual balancing of white and black space.

But I do not show my students the entire page. Instead, I give them the nine separate panels, and I ask them to reassemble these panels into a coherent, meaningful page and to justify their choices. This task asks students to think critically about a complex series of images in terms of narrative, tone, and theme. A reason for this complexity lies in the page itself; it is not simply a matter of reassembling a linear narrative. Because the page is more concerned with establishing both a character's state of mind and a mood of foreboding, the arrangement of the panels does not, for the most part, follow a clearly linear path; thus, the number of possible combinations is extremely high. Students enjoy this activity in no small part because it allows them to be "makers" of meaning, insofar as they become accountable for creative choices. This position is empowering to students, and if they are momentarily disappointed that they don't get it "right," they are relieved to hear that with nine panels, there are over 350,000 different possible combinations. What is more, "right" is relative in this case: the exercise is less about matching Hernandez's choices than it is about the students articulating their own. In fact, not a few students have walked away from this assignment believing that theirs is the superior page.

As with the panel analysis, this assignment is easily adaptable for different grade levels; all that needs to be adjusted is the complexity of the dissembled page or strip. Elementary school teachers, for example, might

Figure 5.2

Copyright 1991 Jaime Hernandez, published by Fantagraphics Books.

cut up newspaper comic strips in order to help students understand the logical flow of a story. Middle and high school teachers could use increasingly complex, age-appropriate comics in a similar manner to help students "see," by their own hand, how images can tell stories and suggest meaning. Regardless of grade level, our students spend much time watching television, playing video games, and surfing the Internet. What we need to do is show them why their critical faculties should likewise be engaged during these visual activities. Many of my students tell me that after one of our class activities they can no longer look at movies or magazine advertisements as they did before, and this comment lets me know that I have been doing my job.

Of course, this analysis is moot if the reading material is not engaging. When we simply show students how to find meaning, the resulting exercises can become odious and rote. What energizes such investigation and helps students become lifelong readers is their interest in the material being studied. I have noticed that students are captivated by this form, and no doubt a key reason lies in our students' attraction to the subversive: "A comic book in English class? Hardcore!"[3] This reaction, in part, prompts some interesting and valuable behavior. When presented with comic books in a classroom setting, my students often read ahead and, more importantly, reread the individual works. It would be difficult to overestimate the importance of these two acts, for they are a clear demonstration not only of student engagement with books, but they also reflect students' acknowledgment that stories are worth revisiting and studying. In an age when getting students to complete the assigned reading is like pushing water uphill, it is energizing to witness them taking the initiative to do extra reading.

Another reason for this engagement is largely attributable to the form itself. Unlike more "traditional" literature, comic books are able to quite literally "put a face" on a given subject; readers "see" the characters through the illustrations, and these characters will often address the reader directly (a common device in comic book autobiography). In addition, reading comic books requires an active, though largely subconscious, participation on the part of the reader, whereby he or she performs "closure . . . [the] phenomenon of observing the parts but perceiving the whole" (McCloud, 1994, p. 63). Because comics are made up of static images, readers must supply, in their own minds, the missing parts. For example, in a page from *Flood*, by Eric Drooker (1992), the protagonist approaches a demonstration on a street corner, and his captivation with the speaker is interrupted by police, who break up the crowd (see Figure 5.3).[4] There is quite a bit that happens in the spaces between the panels—or "in the gutters"—that we are not shown, and yet the missing information does not impede our understanding. For instance, in looking at panels two and three, we do not see our protagonist enter the crowd; in panel two he is outside the circle of people, while in panel three he is within it. In addition, panel five contains in its foreground the partial images—in silhouette, no less—of two figures; despite these figures' minimalist presentation, our minds are still able to "complete" the image by concluding that they are police officers based on the shape of their hats, the sticks that they are holding, and the context of the demonstration. This process of closure is repeated over and over again throughout any given comic, and in this way, comics become a kind of extended gestalt, whereby the reader's mind works continually to complete the picture. The result of this process is "an intimacy . . . between creator and audience" (McCloud, 1994, p. 64). And while all media require some type of closure, no medium depends on it as much as comics. In no small part, the continual closure performed by the reader of a comic book contributes to the form's ability to engage its readers.

Figure 5.3

CONNECTING TO STUDENT LIVES
THROUGH READING AND WRITING

Aside from encouraging students to read and to read meaningfully, another crucial component of a literary literacy that will help our students become lifelong readers is to show them vital connections between literature and their lives. In other words, how can we show students that stories might actually matter to them? The question is endemic to anyone who hopes to be an effective teacher of literature, and without a doubt the question "So what?" reverberates through the minds of many of our students as they slog their way through their assigned reading. Comic books present some unique opportunities to reveal exactly why stories should matter. Like more "traditional" forms of literature, comic books and graphic novels (long comic books, for lack of a better term)[5] address a variety of topics of interest to students and their teachers. There are titles that address history: Art Spiegelman's *Maus I* (1986) and *Maus II* (1992) retell the story of the author's father, a Holocaust survivor. There are titles that address social issues: Judd Winick's *Pedro and Me: Friendship, Loss, and What I Learned* (2000) recounts the author's friendship with Pedro Zamora, a young man who died of AIDS; Katherine Arnoldi's *The Amazing "True" Story of Teenage Single Mom* (1998) provides a frank look at the realities of teen pregnancy and underscores the importance of education. There are titles that chronicle personal growth: Craig Thompson's *Blankets* (2003) is a moving coming-of-age story in which the author retells his troubled relationships with his first love, his artistic gift, and his Christian faith; Marjane Satrapi's *Persepolis I* (2003) and *Persepolis II* (2004) recount, respectively, the author's childhood in Iran and her later education in Europe, providing amazing portraits not only of a culture and its people that rarely make it through to the West, but also of a young girl growing up under adverse conditions. There are titles that enliven myth and fantasy: Neil Gaiman's *Sandman* (1989–1996)[6] is a ten-volume graphic novel that celebrates the importance of stories as it interweaves elements of various mythological and religious traditions, history, popular culture, and even Shakespeare; Bill Willingham's *Fables* (2002–present) is a current series that posits a secret society of living fairy tales who exist in our world; in addition, many superhero titles would be interesting and enlivening complements to units on the hero or mythology. The wealth of choices is impressive.

In fact, it does not take much investigation to find out that this medium fulfills a wide range of our students' reading interests. To get a sense of the depth and breadth of material available, readers need look no further than Stephen Weiner's *The 101 Best Graphic Novels* (2001) or Paul Gravett's *Graphic Novels: Stories to Change Your Life* (2005). Both books are instructive guides through the 10 percent of "non-crud" that Sturgeon alludes to in his law. In addition, there is no shortage of bibliographies on the Internet that list valuable comics and graphic novels, along with suggested age- and reading-level appropriateness. Many of these sites are connected with libraries, which are quickly discovering how deeply students are attracted to this form. I am regularly informed by my own school's librarians that the circulation numbers for the comics and graphic novels in our collection are very high.

Understanding that stories "matter" does not have to depend solely upon reading; students can perceive important connections between literature and life by writing as well, and, here again, comics provide inventive opportunities to make such connections with our students. One such opportunity is the Comic Book Project, developed by Dr. Michael Bitz to help students develop much needed literacy skills through an arts-based project. Specifically, over 700 K–8 students throughout New York City participated in an after-school program where they "brainstormed, outlined, sketched, wrote, and designed original comic books" (Bitz, 2004, p. 574). The project spanned several weeks and was based on the contention that "children discover meaningful dimensions of their worlds when they can explore them through creative arts, including comic books" (Bitz, 2004, p. 575). By creating comic books, students needed to think beyond words to tell their stories; they needed to consider how to represent themselves and their lives in images as well, and thinking in these terms was a productive challenge for them. The results were quite promising. As the projects developed, students showed increasing initiative, or "ownership" of the project, and some students were very reluctant to turn in their final projects, afraid that they would not be returned (Bitz, 2004). Based on researcher-designed exit surveys, the Comic Book Project—which continues today as a program of Teachers College, Columbia University—showed that, in the opinions of both instructors and students, significant progress was realized in several areas, including the students' writing (Bitz, 2004). Just as significant was the realization among the students that their stories are worth telling, that reading and writing are valuable tools that will help them to understand their lives.

Another way to reveal important connections between literature and life is to expose students to literary "communities"—groups that gather in some way to celebrate how stories enrich our lives. The most obvious example of such communities, in terms of "traditional" literature, are reading groups, which have multiplied across the country in recent years (thank you, Oprah). These groups are powerful reinforcements of the value of reading because they offer object lessons in the myriad ways that people find personal value in what they read. More so than any other medium, comic books have a culture of fandom that is so specifically organized and devoted to the form that it is, at times, almost aggressively exclusionary to outsiders. For example, comics are often difficult to find, comics shops tend to be uninviting to the uninitiated, and comic book story lines often require extensive background knowledge of various characters and their past relationships; all of these factors "make it hard for potential casual readers to become interested [in comics]" (Pustz, 1999). One of the unique features of this culture is the communication that takes place between readers and creators, representing a level of accessibility unmatched by other popular media. Such communication takes place in several venues, including online message boards, conventions, and even comic book shops.[7] This communication also takes place within the comic book itself, on the "letters" page. In my class, we spend time examining the letters pages of various comic books, for these letters reveal the rich and varied connections that readers make with stories. Some of these letters fit into the typical "fanboy" mode (e.g., "There's no way that Dr. Strange would have fallen into the cosmic time portal in issue #276 because he already mastered interdimensional travel under the tutelage of the Watcher in issue #250");[8] some offer insightful interpretations of story lines, such as reader Robert Jeschonek's (1986) thoughtful feminist critique of "The Curse" (issue #40 of Alan Moore's landmark run on *Swamp Thing*); and some, like the following—from an issue of *Love and Rockets*—offer heartfelt testimony about how a comic book character can help a reader understand and appreciate his own life experiences.

The writer of this particular letter is a young man who also happens to be gay, and he describes his connection with one of the book's main characters, Maggie, a Hispanic woman who is bisexual:

> I guess I identify with Maggie so much cuz I'm an Iranian guy (a lot of the family stuff seems to be the same as the Mexican thing, as well as the kinda more passionate outlook on life), who got into alternative rock, punk, etc . . . (whatever you wanna call it) when I was 16 which was at the same time as my "coming out"—so the whole attitude really helped shape the way I see things. . . . your comics always seem (to me) to acknowledge the bad stuff without trying to make it better in a phoney [sic] way. BUT also always make me see some of the beauty in the every day things in life— just the way Maggie walks down the street to buy sweets or comics, or that nervous excitement of going to a live music show, or having a burger late at night, or the effort Maggie's putting into something so boring but so important as helping her tenants with their air-conditioning, even if they don't really show their appreci- ation . . . I dunno, you just make me remember that these little things and these experiences we barely pay attention to are so important and so beautiful. (Shamsavari, 2002, p. 31)

It is difficult to read these lines and not be moved by the ways in which the stories in *Love and Rockets* have enriched this particular reader's life. As such, this and other letters—unique artifacts of comic book culture—can serve as powerful examples to our students that reading matters.

INVITING ACTIVE LITERACY LEARNING

The final requirement of fostering a literary literacy that encourages lifelong reading is to invite our students to take a more active role in their literary education. With every nonreflective presentation of canonical literature, we indirectly encourage student passivity and, perhaps, resentment. As teachers of literature, we should not strive to get students to accept without question our own (or others') judgments of what constitutes literary merit because such acceptance inevitably places students in the position of seeing literature as a "medicine" that will somehow make them better people, if only they learn to appreciate it. When students view literature in this light, they develop biases against it, and while they may learn to read, they do not develop a passion for reading. Instead, teachers need to address the very issue of literary merit, for the resulting dialogue can help shape and legitimize the students' own voices in articulating their literary judgments—something that is necessary if one is to become a lifelong reader. Some important questions that need to be asked about canon formation are: "What is considered 'literature'?" "What is not?" "Who decides this?" "What are their interests?" Many of our students may not have considered asking these questions before, but as they do, they begin to engage in the more active practice of cultural production, as opposed to cultural reproduction, which "anesthetizes one's capacity to think independently and critically" (Macedo, 2003, p. 13). That is, by engaging with these questions, students are not simply regurgitating our own opinions back at us; instead, they are forming their own. And in so doing, they begin to see literary study—and literature—not as something to be feared, but as something to which they can make a contribution.

Comic books invite our students to make such contributions precisely because their very presence begs the question, "What is literature?" That is, most people are not convinced that comic books have any literary value; in fact, most people are not convinced that they have any value whatsoever, aside from the money paid by collectors for rare issues. Because comics are generally held in such disregard, students find them more approachable and are thus more willing to make comments about literary quality. The ensuing conversation then becomes an ideal way to begin asking vital questions about canon formation. Having taught comic books alongside more "traditional" forms of literature, I can attest that when asked to critically evaluate a comic book, students are much more forthcoming with their ideas and opinions than they are during a classroom discussion of works such as Faulkner's "Barn Burning" or Alice Walker's *The Color Purple*. Too often, students perceive such works as occupying a space above their level of thought, and the important question of why or by whom these works were deemed "literary" never comes up. The fact is simply—and uncritically—accepted. And even if students ultimately reject the idea that comic books are literature, as some of them no doubt will, to do so requires that they think about the issue, their own definitions of "literariness," and the work itself in a more critical way than if they simply accepted—or pretended to accept—our own views and biases. In effect, by using comic books to open a dialogue with students about what constitutes "literature," teachers enact a powerful lesson for students about the importance of voicing one's opinions, and, as a result, students are more likely to participate in the dialogue rather than fall asleep during it.[9]

Participation is valuable because it usually leads to more participation; students will speak up when they feel that their classroom is a place where all ideas will be considered. Comic books allow teachers to demonstrate this principle because their very presence as an object of study implies that we should not make assumptions that might deny us access to wonderful worlds of literary possibilities. As I hope I have made clear throughout this chapter, I am not one of those advocates for comic books who damns them with the faint praise that they are useful in getting kids to read "real" books. Regardless of popular perceptions, comic books and graphic novels can be every bit as complicated, challenging, and enlightening as more traditional literary forms, and they certainly hold a prominent place on this lifelong reader's bookshelves. I like to remind students that these popular perceptions concerning the relative value of a particular genre, while powerful, are also known to change. Most students are surprised to learn that both film and the novel were once judged as "trash" forms and dismissed as not at all "literary." They are especially surprised about the latter genre, given that the lion's share of what they now consider to be literature is, in fact, made up of novels. Unfortunately, people make such judgments and dismissals, based on incomplete understanding, not only about works of literature, but about individuals and groups, as well. These judgments are often directed at many of our students who might feel marginalized for reasons of ethnicity, academic preparation, socioeconomic class, or a host of other factors that impact self-perceptions. No doubt some of our own students have, at one time or another, felt unfairly judged on the basis of appearances, and they may find some metaphoric resonance in the plight of comic books in America. And as teachers, we can be sure to amplify this resonance so that it is not to be missed.

In these days of measurable outcomes, state standards, and No Child Left Behind, the act of bringing comic books into a K–12 classroom is risky business. And yet, teaching is all about risk because the stakes are so high. The bottom line is that teaching a child to read is not enough. We lifelong readers do not read simply because we can; we read because our spirit depends on it. The question, of course, is how to lead our students to this realization, and I believe that the answer lies, in part, with comic books. My conviction on this matter was formed, ironically, in that same class where my students first attempted in vain to recall some book that meant something to them. Later in the year we read Chester Brown's (1994) comic book memoir *I Never Liked You*, which is ostensibly about Brown's adolescent interactions with various girls but is also a subtle meditation on the nature of language and silence and the complications between sons and mothers. The story is told very matter-of-factly, and Brown's tone, coupled with his understated artistic style, lends his story a mature, restrained power. The students were entertained and engaged by some of the other pieces we read—all prose—but with Brown, the reactions were of a markedly different nature. For one thing, the students were completely pulled into Brown's story. Most students had read the book two or more times, and they conversed and argued energetically with each other about the story's various characters, situations, and ideas. On our first day of discussion, in fact, students were already talking about the book when I walked into the classroom: What should Chester have done? Why didn't he act? Why did he have such trouble with words? Why can words be so troublesome? We went around and around on these and other questions, and I found that my students were doing most of the talking. It was the classroom as true conversation, an occurrence that should be much more common in education than it is. And second, many of my students were surprised by their own degree of involvement. They wondered how such simply rendered words and pictures could move them so completely. In retrospect, I had accomplished the goal of leading my students toward literary literacy when one young woman held up her copy of *I Never Liked You* and asked, "Are there more books like this around?"

NOTES

1. Today, the Comics Code is largely irrelevant, but at the time, it was quite serious. In effect, if a publisher wanted to sell a particular comic book at either a newsstand, drugstore, or grocery store, then the book needed to have the imprimatur of the Comics Code—the "Seal of Approval." At the time, these retail locations represented the only venue in which to sell a comic book. Thus, if a comic did not conform to the strictures of the Code, then for all intents and purposes it could not be sold. It was not until the 1980s, when comic book shops emerged in great numbers, that the Code became obsolete. These shops were not tied to the Code and became the new primary market for comic book publishers.

2. Happily, popular perception of comic books is changing, albeit gradually. Ever since the mid-1980s, comic books have been gaining—though modestly, to be sure—some measure of respectability. Books like Alan Moore's *Watchmen* (1986) and Frank Miller's *The Dark Knight Returns* (1986) reinvigorated the mainstream market by overlaying maturity and sly self-knowing atop genre conventions. Art Spiegelman's *Maus* I (1986) and *Maus II* (1992)—the author's story of his father, a Holocaust survivor—showed that this medium could tell effective stories about people who did not wear capes. The latter book, in fact, won a Pulitzer Prize for that year. Of late, more and more comic book writers and comic books have garnered attention from the mainstream media. Reviews of comics and graphic novels have been featured in such publications as *The New York Times Book Review*, *Time*, *Entertainment Weekly*, and *Rolling Stone*. In addition, while one need only

look at year-end box office grosses to see that numerous film adaptations are being made of mainstream superhero comics, what might be less apparent is that independent comics are receiving attention as well: Two critically acclaimed movies of the last five years—*Ghost World* (2000) and *American Splendor* (2003)—are based on such comics. In short, the comic book still has a long way to go to escape its popular conception as immature, but its deserved position as a legitimate artistic and literary form is being established.

3. Comics are all about the subversive. Long before Edward Murrow took Joe McCarthy to task, the Wisconsin senator and his witch hunts were being harshly satirized by Walt Kelly in his comic strip *Pogo*, which was syndicated nationwide in newspapers published by the very conservative Hearst Corporation. Also in the 1950s, during the Korean War, EC Comics published *Two-Fisted Tales* and *Frontline Combat* (both under the editorship of Harvey Kurtzman)—two series of war comics that undermined the dominant ideology of the time by taking an anti-war stance, humanizing the enemy, and criticizing U.S. policy. Later, in the 1960s, several comic book artists (some of whom were inspired by *MAD* magazine, another Kurtzman creation) would begin an "underground" comics movement that dovetailed with the underground press to blast various social, political, and moral taboos. It is precisely because people do not take comics seriously that artists and writers in this medium are able to "sneak in" controversial topics. I have yet to meet a student who would not be intrigued by this situation.

4. I use *Flood* because students tend to admire his expressive, woodcut style; teachers could use virtually any page from any comic book to illustrate this principle.

5. To a large extent, I use the terms "comic book" and "graphic novel" somewhat interchangeably. In many cases, graphic novels are long stories or story arcs that represent a collection of individual comic books, which told the story in a serialized form. In other cases, graphic novels are original publications, having never appeared before in the comic book form. This latter situation was once pretty rare, but is now becoming more common. In terms of the unique poetics of comics, which I reference at various points in this chapter, there is no difference between the two forms. In terms of connotations and physical properties, however, there are important differences. For one thing, graphic novels are more "acceptable" forms of reading—particularly by adults; the word "novel" calls to mind the form of choice for Dickens, Wharton, and Hemingway—you know, "real" literature. In addition, bookstores prefer to carry graphic novels over comics because, in part, they have a thick spine, sit nicely upon a shelf, and, overall, look more like "real" books. On a recent trip to Borders—which, much to its credit, carries both graphic novels and comic books—I saw that the former group had their own bookshelf while the latter were on a wire rack with the magazines (other "disposable" reading). There are, however, important features of a comic book that are not present in a graphic novel. One of these features, which I discuss later in this chapter, is the "letters" column—a forum in which readers write in to a particular comic book's creator(s). When individual comic books are collected into a graphic novel, these columns are the first to be jettisoned, as are the advertisements, which are valuable for cultural critics who use comic books as part of their materials. In a later section of this chapter, I list some particular titles that might be of interest to teachers and students, and those titles are graphic novels. I cite these for one main reason: The graphic-novel versions are the ones that will be most accessible

commercially to interested readers. Books remain in print; comic books wind up in dusty "back issues" boxes in hard-to-find comic book stores.

6. *Sandman* had the distinction of being the only mainstream comic book with nearly as many female as male readers (Bender, 1999).

7. One of the most distinctive features of this culture is that it is highly participatory. Readers routinely connect with writers and artists in extensive discussions of stories, and more than once, readers of comic books have influenced the directions of stories, even going so far as to determine the fate (or return) of a particular character. The most notable (and notorious) example of reader influence is Jim Starlin's *Batman: A Death in the Family* (1988). The story was originally serialized in four issues, and at one point, Robin (the Boy Wonder) was captured by the Joker. The comic's publisher, DC, made the decision to set up two phone numbers that readers could call to decide Robin's fate: one number would let him live, and the other would let him die. In a perverse unmasking of the fan community, Robin received (by a slim margin) the "thumbs down."

8. Okay, I made this up. But it's certainly representative of the spirit of many of the comments on letters pages in mainstream comics.

9. Clearly, a delicate balance exists between passing on our own literary judgments and encouraging our students to develop their own, and this balance is especially precarious in the K–12 classroom, where students first need exposure to literature before they can be in a position to argue literary merit. Thus, teachers at these grade levels are faced with the significant challenge of presenting literature in a way that at once interests students, presents some model of literary evaluation, convinces students that such evaluation is important, and leaves them room in which to develop their own model. Creating such a classroom is not easy—especially when we consider that students will carry the attitudes they form in these early courses for a long time—but as I argue throughout this chapter, well-chosen comic books and graphic novels can help with these tasks.

REFERENCES

Bender, H. (1999). *The sandman companion.* New York: Vertigo/DC Comics.

Benton, M. (1993). *The comic book in America.* Dallas: Taylor Publishing.

Bitz, M. (2004). The comic book project: Forging alternative pathways to literacy. *Journal of Adolescent and Adult Literacy, 47*(7), 574–586.

Brown, C. (1994). *I never liked you: A comic book.* Montreal, Canada: Drawn & Quarterly.

Burmark, L. (2002). *Visual literacy: Learn to see, see to learn.* Alexandria, VA: Association for Supervision and Curriculum Development.

Bustle, L. S. (2004). The role of visual representation in the assessment of learning. *Journal of Adolescent and Adult Literacy, 47*(5), 416–423.

Cadiero-Kaplan, K. (2002). Literacy ideologies: Critically engaging the language arts curriculum. *Language Arts, 79*(5), 372–381.

Drooker, E. (1992). *Flood: A novel in pictures.* New York: Four Walls Eight Windows Press.

Giddins, G. (2004). Seduced by Classics Illustrated. In Sean Howe (Ed.), *Give our regards to the atomsmashers: Writers on comics* (pp. 78–94). New York: Pantheon.

Greco, N. (1992). Critical literacy and community service: Reading and writing the world. *English Journal, 81*(5), 83–85.

Hernandez, J. (1991). "Flies on the ceiling." In *Flies on the Ceiling: Volume Nine of the Complete Love and Rockets* (pp. 1–15). Seattle: Fantagraphics.

Hoffmann, G. (2000). Visual literacy needed in the 21st century. *ETC,* Summer, 219–222.

Jeschonek, R. (1986). Letter. *Swamp Thing #46.* New York: DC Comics.

Macedo, D. (2003). Literacy matters. *Language Arts, 81*(1), 12–14.

McCloud, S. (1994). *Understanding comics.* New York: HarperCollins.

Nyberg, A. K. (1998). *Seal of approval: The history of the comics code.* Jackson, MS: University of Mississippi Press.

Oring, S. (2000). A call for visual literacy. *School Arts, 4,* 58–59.

Perloff, M. (May 9, 1997). A passion for content: Restoring "literary literacy" to the English curriculum. *Chronicle of Higher Education,* B4–B5.

Pustz, M. (1999). *Comic book culture: Fanboys and true believers.* Jackson, MS: University of Mississippi Press.

Sabin, R. (1993). *Adult comics.* New York: Routledge.

Shamsavari, S. (2002). Letter. *Love and Rockets.* Summer 2002, 31.

Simons, T. (2002). Preface. In L. Burmark, *Visual literacy: Learn to see, see to learn.* Alexandria, VA: Association for Supervision and Curriculum Development.

Sturgeon's Law. (n.d.). *Cool jargon of the day.* Retrieved November 7, 2005, from http://www.jargon.net/jargonfile/s/SturgeonsLaw.html

Sturm, J. (2001). *The golem's mighty swing.* Montreal: Drawn and Quarterly.

Whittaker, P. (2001, October). What's the point of fiction in a world of trouble? *New Internationalist, 339,* 9–12.

Witek, J. (1989). *Comic books as history.* Jackson: University of Mississippi.

Yoon, J. C. (2001). Literacy practices in dark times: A reflective memoir. *Journal of Adolescent and Adult Literacy, 45*(4), 290–294.

6

That's Funny

Political Cartoons in the Classroom

Thomas DeVere Wolsey

What do political cartoons offer in support of visual literacy develop-ment? Wolsey analyzes one cartoonist's work to offer a lens for under-standing the visual elements necessary to make meaning. In addition, he provides teachers with insights into how political cartoons can be used in the classroom to foster learning.

Among my earliest memories are those where I sat with my father while he read the morning paper. Often, the family mutt would pull at Dad's socks while we read the comic pages. I do not remember the front page or the obituaries, but the memories of cartoons and reading with my father stay with me still. Cartoon images are intuitively appealing. The visual information captures instantly what thousands of words may only approximate. I am sure that I don't have to recite a well-known cliché about the relative worth of a picture as measured in a thousand words to elicit a memory of a cartoon or comic in the reader's mind (Gillespie, 1993). Consider the visual impact of the Matson cartoon (Figure 6.1) that appeared in the *New York Observer* after the attacks on the World Trade Center in 2001. Cartoons often connote a humorous and light-hearted

Figure 6.1

Reprinted with permission from Cagle Cartoons Inc. www.cagle.com.

approach to the subject matter at hand. However, readers who recall the devastation at the Pentagon, the World Trade Center, and the downed flight over Pennsylvania will immediately recognize the artfulness in Matson's cartoon.[1]

Neither funny nor light-hearted, the cartoon precisely captured what it meant for many to be an American on September 11, 2001.

Readers of an American newspaper expect that journalists capture the essence of a newsworthy event or personality dispassionately; audiences of a newspaper prefer at least the illusion of verity from reporters. Objectivity, that elusive target, is the hallmark of the news reporter. The editors of the opinion and editorial pages are singularly free from that criterion, however. And, it can be argued that the political cartoonist is the least constrained of all. Political cartoonists capture emotions and aesthetics in ways that the facts of a news story cannot. When they are well done, political cartoons can trap human moments, with all the complexities that make humans what they are, in time and in two-dimensional space. Where a news story might make a reader shake his or her head, either yea or nay, at what fellow humans have done, a political cartoon can render a reader speechless, invoking an ironic smile, a tear, or a flush of anger.

The terms "political cartoon" and "editorial cartoon" are used interchangeably in most contexts. While the terms are not exactly synonymous, we will not differentiate between them here. Such cartoons exaggerate features of persons and events in order to draw attention to important characteristics that illustrate the subject's essence. Lamb (2004) suggests that political cartoonists may have captured, better than other journalists, the most realistic version of the 2000 presidential election, where the contest between Bush and Gore began in the most mundane of ways but ended with a close race that, whatever the reader's political leanings, might best be described as absurd: "If ever an election was of the cartoonists, by the cartoonists, and for the cartoonists, this was it" (pp. 57–58). Political cartoonist Daryl Cagle compared written columns and illustrations: "Expressing an opinion in a picture is much more elegant" (personal interview, January 6, 2006).

THE POLITICAL CARTOON

We can differentiate by their purposes the comics I read with my father from the political cartoons most often found on the opinion and editorial pages. Political cartoonists think of themselves as journalists and graphic commentators (Cagle, personal interview, January 6, 2006). While comic strips entertain and even cause us to reflect on important issues, Jay Evensen, editor of the editorial pages at the Salt Lake City *Deseret Morning News*, believes that political cartoons are becoming increasingly funny while comics are increasingly political (personal interview, January 20, 2006).

The political cartoon focuses on the power relations and deployment of authority within and between groups. In Figure 6.1, consider the knife in Lady Liberty's back; Liberty may represent one group while the knife represents another, more nebulous political group in this cartoon. The symbolized groups can be families, neighborhoods, nations, or a planet. The noted historian Howard Zinn (1999) argues that the more the public appears to control the mechanisms of the state, the more subtle, sophisticated, and difficult to detect are the measures of control that the state must take. The role of public discourse in both keeping watch on government and monitoring our own public and private relationships is always a primary consideration in a democratic society. In the public sphere, people might grapple rationally with the dichotomies of the space where private and public interests collide. Political cartoons are artifacts that reside in the realm of this public sphere if we let them. The catch, of course, in working in such a space is that one must initially, if temporarily, set aside one's own views in order to understand those of others. Only from such an understanding can a productive and rational debate proceed. Evensen (personal interview, January 20, 2006) suggested that those who take exception to the cartoons the *Deseret Morning News* prints often have failed to look beyond the image itself or to challenge their own biases.

Political cartoons may appear deceptively simple. When we view a political cartoon, our first reaction is often emotional. However, a good cartoon requires that we spend a bit more time with it than a first glance and initial reaction. With that idea in mind, given all the words on the editorial pages that require cognitive effort, the cartoonist wants to hit the reader over the head with an idea (Cagle, personal interview, January 6, 2006). "Blast you with it," were his actual words. Perhaps if students don't have the background they need in order to be "blasted with" the ideas represented in the cartoon, and if that background can't be constructed within the time constraints of school calendars and students' attention spans, the teacher should instead select a different image and move on. So, we are at the point where we must ask ourselves just what role political cartoons play in the public spaces we all must inhabit and how students might productively engage with this primarily visual tool.

Political cartoons are a window on current events and a bridge across time to historical events. Like other literacy tasks, teachers should look beyond the content and consider the cognitive skills students need to make sense of the world of the political cartoon. In a few pen strokes, political cartoonists must capture highly complex events and personalities. To do this, they make use of symbols, metaphors, analogies, and exaggerations. They ask the reader or viewer of cartoons to identify similarities and differences and to infer causality, consequences, and relationships. Later in this chapter, we will examine a historical cartoon using these cognitive tools. Cartoons require the reader to be observant and aware of what is going on in the world beyond the school walls. They challenge the reader to question the power structures and ensure that public dialogue remains a democratic function.

With all of these cognitive feats waiting to be unfolded from the political cartoon and the attendant possibility of encouraging students to think deeply about a world that can be deeply troubled, the cartoon offers hope that tomorrow will be better. To locate that hope, the teacher must help students identify their first emotional responses, and then ponder, consider, and reflect on what else might be found there. Embedded in the cartoon are images, and within those images there are symbols, metaphors, and cultural references. Evensen told me that there are two aspects to the political cartoon: the image and the message (personal interview, January 20, 2006). An image can overwhelm a message if the cultural background is so strong that the cartoonist's message is lost, but at the same time a message may not be apparent if the irony is not suggested strongly enough by the image. Students, most of whom are novices at the art of the visual metaphor, require teachers to help them identify sophisticated thinking. Teachers, as experts, must be critical readers and viewers of the news and of sophisticated thinking that may go outside the boundaries of the teacher's own opinions.

Confronted with the difficulties of engaging students with the arguably difficult content of the political cartoon, teachers can take heart.

A 1999 study of civic attitudes held by fourteen-year-olds showed that American ninth-graders compared favorably with students overall in twenty-seven other countries and that they had a higher than average expectation of engaging as citizens in a democracy in the future (National Center for Education Statistics, 2001). If the public as a whole seems politically polarized, disengaged, or both, our students do care about their government, the society in which they live, and the future they will inhabit.

The teachers' responsibilities include working out how things that matter to a larger world might also matter to third- or twelfth-graders: "If it doesn't matter to students, it doesn't matter" (Wink, 2005, p. 173). I don't think that when Joan Wink wrote this that she meant that teachers should teach only those things that students say matter. The political cartoon in the classroom challenges the teacher with working out how things matter to their students. It also presents the opportunity for students to find what matters to them and what might matter to a larger segment of society, as well.

WHAT SHOULD STUDENTS BE ABLE TO DO? WHAT IS THE TEACHER'S ROLE?

Students should be able to analyze a primary-source document. Technically, a primary-source document is one that was created by a participant or witness to what happened in the past; current political cartoons are close cousins (they will soon be historical documents). If we push the definition a bit, the cartoonist is an observer in the midst of events as they unfold, and we can use the cognitive tools of the historian to encourage and to scaffold the work we ask students to do with images, particularly political cartoons. Of course, our purpose is to focus on how best to assist students in understanding political cartoons, rather than to pursue the debate of what is or is not a primary-source document. Tally and Goldenberg's (2005) suggestions for the sort of historical thinking about documents can also be applied more widely to the political cartoon. We will call this model Cartoon Thinking (Table 6.1).

Table 6.1   Cartoon Thinking

- Observe the document's features
- Use prior knowledge
- Speculate about causes and consequences
- Make personal connections
- Use evidence to support speculation

Since a student's world doesn't always include wide knowledge of the details of current events or the experience to recognize many of the symbols or analogies that might be present in a political cartoon, teachers have the additional responsibility of helping students with the background knowledge or schemata (Bartlett, 1932) they need to make sense of the political cartoon's graphic statement. Teachers have long known that what is done prior to a traditional reading in a textbook or novel is critical to student success in actually reading the text (e.g., Betts, 1946; Dechant, 1991; Ryder & Graves, 2003). The same is true when a teacher uses a political cartoon.

Beyond the cartoon's topic and requisite background knowledge of that topic, teachers must also attend to the visual inferences, analogies, symbols, and metaphors that the cartoonist has employed. Many newspaper readers can probably think of a time when a political cartoon they viewed didn't make sense to them. This doesn't mean the cartoon wasn't a successful one, but it does suggest that the reader might have missed a news story that was of importance to the cartoonist. When students examine historical cartoons, there is a possibility they will lack the background knowledge needed to create an understanding of the images, especially given the intricacies of interrelated historical events, the complexity of symbols, analogies, and so forth. Teachers who know what a symbol might mean, such as a Republican elephant or Democratic donkey, shouldn't assume that students will, too. It might help some students if cartoons are paired with a related news story.

Some questions about what cartoons to use and when to use them are also appropriate. Rulli (2003) proposed a series of questions that can guide teachers in choosing documents to be used in social science classrooms. We will choose and modify three that can be adapted as guides for teachers as they select and incorporate political cartoons into their curricula.

1. Does an examination of the cartoon lead to larger issues or concepts of study?

2. Does the cartoon have immediate or potential relevance for students?

3. Do students have the requisite background knowledge to interpret and understand the cartoon?

One approach to graphic information asks teachers to help students determine what graphic information is presented, to assist them in synthesizing the information presented with other knowledge (in the case of political cartoons, other news sources provide critical comparison information), and to facilitate reinforcing and applying that information in new ways (Reinking, 1988). Both Reinking's graphic information lesson model and Rulli's (2003) criteria for selecting documents require that students access prior knowledge and connect that knowledge and knowledge of the graphic or cartoon at hand to other information. Evensen proposes that students need to be aware of current events in order to make sense of political cartoons (personal interview, January 20, 2006). Thus, the process of thinking about political cartoons is recursive; viewers might be encouraged to read the news in order to make sense of the political cartoons, and political cartoons might encourage viewers to read more of the news.

A CLASSROOM EXAMPLE: THOMAS NAST

A cartoon by Thomas Nast from *Harper's Weekly* situates our discussion of political cartoons within the classroom. Thomas Nast is arguably the most recognizable political cartoonist in American journalism. It may be a disservice to examine a single work, particularly of a figure like Nast, outside of the context of his entire oeuvre (Justice, 2005). However, one cartoon will assist us in finding an appropriate way to use the political cartoon in the twenty-first-century classroom. This particular cartoon appeared just prior to the death of Ulysses S. Grant (see Figure 6.2). Imagine a group of

Figure 6.2

SOURCE: *Harper's Weekly* [Our Ulysses: April 9, 1865—A never forgotten deed]

students discussing this cartoon using the framework for Cartoon Thinking, provided above.

Observe the document's features. In examining the features of this cartoon, students will readily see the U.S. Capitol in the background. A female figure stands, arms stretched upward, behind a man wearing what appears to be Greek clothing from the classical period. At the man's feet we see another man, but this man is clearly of African descent and is bowing down. All three figures in the cartoon stand or kneel on a precipice overlooking a great chasm.

Use background knowledge. Taking time to examine the features and details of the artwork is useful, but this is only a beginning. Next, teachers using this cartoon would need to assist students as they probe what they already know about its features. What students don't know or can't infer on their own or without help, they should be told. The man in the foreground is Ulysses S. Grant, and students may recognize him because of his facial features. That's prior knowledge (Fisher & Wolsey, in press). If students don't know who the character in the visual represents, the teacher should tell students who the man is. But why is he wearing the clothing of an ancient Greek citizen instead of his famously disheveled general's uniform from the U.S. Civil War? Well, students may recall from other lessons that, at least in the popular imagination, Greeks were known as aggressive warriors. Students, with help from their teachers, can infer that Grant certainly had in common the aggressive military bearing that was a primary cause of the Union's successes in the latter years of the war.

Now, who is that lady behind Grant? Students may think of the Statue of Liberty. Lady Liberty is the personification of freedom, and she is a symbol. She is often depicted with an arm raised upward. If students can use the Internet to retrieve images of Liberty, they will find that she often carries a sword, but it is almost always pointed downward. In this cartoon, both arms are raised up. Does that mean something?

Students should also be taught to determine what prior knowledge they lack, that is, existing holes in their knowledge. Such a thoughtful approach leads to questions that can help the viewer of the cartoon. Our imaginary students, and the reader's real students, may wonder why the man who championed the Union and delivered emancipation proclamations to slave populations throughout the South would have an African American kneeling at his feet. People kneel in prayer, to propose marriage, and as servants. Given time, opportunity, and encouragement, students might also realize that people kneel in gratitude, and that must be the correct inference for the kneeling figure in this cartoon.

Thinking about causes and consequences. In the Nast cartoon, several causes are evident, too. First, the kneeling African American could be perceived as grateful for Grant's role as a liberator. In other words, causality of liberation can be ascribed to Grant symbolically. An observant student might also consider that, even though Nast championed radical Republican views of his time, there could also be buried racism there, too. After all, why isn't the African American figure standing next to Grant instead of kneeling at his feet? The U.S. Capitol appears in this cartoon. Students might speculate that it represents a restored union preserved by Grant's actions. They might also speculate that the failure of Congress to grapple with American ideals of justice and equality and the peculiar institution of slavery resulted in war, but that war resulted in the preservation of the Union. Such a discussion can and should be rich and varied, and there are many more meanings that can be explicated from Nast's cartoon than are presented here. The value of discussing a carefully chosen political cartoon in assisting students to reflect on and transform their understanding of distant historical facts should now be clear, however.

Making personal connections. Students whose teachers bring political cartoons to the classroom for the purpose of learning about the world and the people who inhabit it (rather than for the purpose of reinforcing a particular or singular point of view) make use of a learning cycle identified first by Kurt Lewin and described by David Kolb (1984) (Figure 6.3).

Figure 6.3

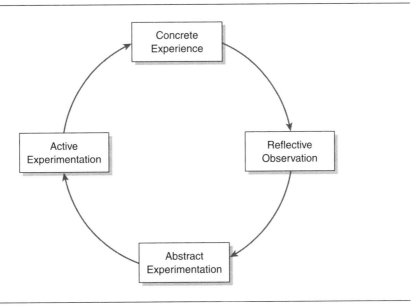

SOURCE: Kolb, David A., *Experiential learning: Experience as a source of learning,* © 1984, p. 21. Adapted with permission of Pearson Education, Inc., Upper Saddle River, NJ.

In this model, students take the visual information of the cartoon and reflect on it using the Cartoon Thinking framework described earlier. To make personal connections, students must work back and forth within the cycle to see what concepts such as liberty, union, or equality might mean in historical context and to the twenty-first-century student.

Without the opportunity to connect and transform knowledge through the process of abstract conceptualization, a student (or a teacher) might think of the Civil War as just another historical event. Reflection allows a personal connection that is more than just a nice way to keep kids motivated. Instead, reflection allows those personal connections to be transformed into abstractions. Abstraction is the process whereby we can simultaneously connect with the events and people of the past, in the present, and think about what that might mean for the future. Here, students might ask something like, "Do we need someone like Ulysses S. Grant today in the twenty-first century?" It's better if a student can work with the abstraction that produces such a question rather than have only the teacher pose the questions. If the teacher poses the question, the students may not have transformed the knowledge themselves; there is no personal connection. Students can simultaneously wonder why Grant, having succeeded in war, is still standing on a precipice; they can also wonder if they and their peers stand on a similar precipice today.

Follow the evidence. In the Nast cartoon, as with any abstraction, it is important for students to think about why they know what they know. How do students know that is Lady Liberty behind Grant? How do they know that the African American is actually kneeling in gratitude rather than servitude? Asking such questions and answering them keeps students on track and leads to better questions of the students' own. It is fine for students to push back against the sources they encounter (and perhaps they should), but they should be familiar with the texts, images, and authorities who otherwise would interpret historical events for them. Finally, while teachers are experts in their disciplines, students are novices. The teacher can point out what features of the cartoon, and of the news to which it refers, are important.

Earlier, it was suggested that taking just one image of Nast's from his oeuvre would not be the best use of the cartoon. For example, Nast frequently included the Lady Liberty figure in his cartoons; the more students see those nineteenth-century images, the more conversant they will be with the ideals that Nast attempted to convey in his art. Indeed, we might teach students not just to refer to the current chapter of the textbook, but to think of many other cartoons and images they've unfolded. Putting a single work in context explains the human events and relationships both in Nast's (or any other cartoonist's) eyes and in our own eyes.

POLITICAL CARTOONS AS MEDIATING TOOLS

The important thing about the experiential learning model in Figure 6.3 is that the more learners engage with content, with ideas, and with their teachers and peers, the more motivated to do so they become. Veteran social studies teacher John Little believes that, as the school year goes by, students become increasingly proficient at thinking about political cartoons, and they like it more (personal interview, January 7, 2006). In addition, he says the students tend to watch the news more at home in order to participate in classroom discussions. The political cartoon becomes a tool to mediate critical thought as a process and as a product expected of educated citizens.

THAT'S A GOOD QUESTION

How teachers choose to employ questions to foster discussion is at least as important as what questions they choose. In Figure 6.4, Cagle has suggested that perhaps the venerated space shuttle should be retired. On the Cagle.com teacher pages, Cynthia Kirkeby (2005) has proposed some questions that challenge students to look critically at the cartoon, bring

Figure 6.4

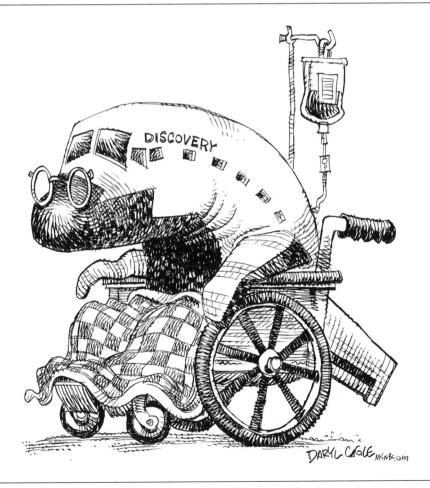

SOURCE: Reprinted with permission from Cagle Cartoons Inc. www.cagle.com

their own knowledge of the space shuttle missions forward, and think about what that means currently and in the future. None of these questions dwell only on the events of the news story that prompted the cartoon (see Table 6.2).

Table 6.2   Kirkeby's Questions: Elderly Space Shuttle

Has the space-shuttle program become too obsolete and dangerous to continue?

Does the space program need a new goal, such as a manned mission to Mars?

Would the current space missions be better accomplished through unmanned, remotely controlled space flights?

COMPARISON

Comparison is a cognitive skill that permits the viewer to use a kind of lens to illuminate aspects of the world that might otherwise remain hidden or at least obscure. In viewing a political cartoon, the viewer must bring together what is known about the topic and compare that against a vast store of background knowledge. Sometimes that background knowledge can be another cartoon. Immediately after September 11, 2001, cartoonists responded with memorial cartoons that attempted to capture the emotions of many. The Matson cartoon (Figure 6.1) at the beginning of this chapter is an example of a memorial cartoon. Using the image-search features of popular search engines, students might compare the cartoon with other cartoons just after September 11, 2001. However, compare Matson's cartoon with Cagle's cartoon published a year later (Figure 6.5).

The visual metaphor in this cartoon is compelling on its own. But when compared with the memorial cartoon in Figure 6.1, students have a lens through which they can examine how the public responds to such a devastating tragedy over time and to others in the historical past. Such a unique view of American culture would be difficult to attain with any other medium, and putting the two cartoons side-by-side affords a new and singular view. Political cartoonists often make viewers, and editors, uncomfortable; sometimes a cartoon image is more than a little ahead of current public opinion (Lamb, 2004). In comparing cartoons on the same topic from two different times, a culture (and its students) can critically examine itself in the mirror. Students immersed

Figure 6.5

in the culture might initially take offense at the 9/11 commercialization cartoon, but placed in context with another cartoon the context may cause introspection.

Cartoons invite us to think critically about ourselves, but they also afford students the opportunity to think about the medium of cartooning, too. Cartoons can help bridge the gap between what students as novices know and what a well-informed reader of the news and of society knows. In Figure 6.6, Cagle turns his pen toward his fellow cartoonists who responded with clichés to the anthrax attacks and subsequent scares in September and October of 2001 because the topic was so ubiquitous. This cartoon uses satire to ask the viewer to consider the impact of terrorism in a country that didn't know the phenomenon firsthand and to lampoon cartoons that relied too heavily on cultural metaphors that become so common the message is homogenized and accepted as received knowledge.

Since political cartoons encourage us to consider other viewpoints, students may want to search the Internet for cartoons that represent differing

Figure 6.6

SOURCE: Reprinted with permission from Cagle Cartoons Inc. www.cagle.com

points of view on the same topic. WorldPress.org archives news, including political cartoons (http://www.worldpress.org/cartoons.cfm), from around the world, offering students a window onto other perspectives that a single news source alone might fail to provide. NewspaperIndex.com (http://www.newspaperindex.com/en/) provides links to newspapers with an online presence from around the world, and many of these newspapers are also available in English.

RAISE YOUR HAND IF
YOU HAVE SOMETHING TO SAY

Classroom discussion is a time-honored teaching technique, but teachers who are truly good at it know that it takes more than just saying, "What do you think?" Traditional recitation structures that often pass for dialogue place the teacher at the center of discussion. Effective dialogue in the classroom, however, is the result of instructional planning, and it must recognize the value of what students have to contribute, as well (Tharp & Gallimore, 1989). Dialogue, it may be argued, is beholden to what has been said before and also considers what might be said in the future (Cheyne & Tarulli, 1999). Political cartoons offer a tool that requires students to consider what events occurred before the cartoon was drawn while considering what might be said later in the conversation. Further, they build on the emotive reaction that visual metaphors can achieve and invite the students participating in the conversation to add to the communally constructed understanding.

DRAW, PARTNER

Professional artists who draw political cartoons employ an array of cognitive tools, and so can students. Students who struggle to make sense of the complex world of politics, government, and culture might also draw political cartoons in order to make sense of that world. Drawings can make explicit ideas that are complex and make visible what is hidden. Students do not need to be proficient artists; instead they may focus on getting an idea across using some of the cartoonists' tools and techniques, for example, use of symbols, exaggeration, visual metaphor, and so on. Creating an image may be considered a form of visual summarization (Fisher & Wolsey, in press). Electronic media increase the options students have in creating effective visuals acceptable for instructional purposes (Rakes, 1999).

One strategy might be to ask students to draw a political cartoon on a topic that is either assigned or student-selected (McConnell, 1992; Rakes, 1999). Students then share their drawings with peers and small groups. They explain why they know what they know about the topic that has been incorporated into the drawing. Next, the teacher asks students to read more about that topic from a news source and discuss their new understanding. The students integrate that new understanding into the drawing by either revising it or completing a new cartoon. Finally, students go back to their groups with *before* and *after* drawings and explain the alterations that were made and why those alterations were necessary.

Students may initially have a difficult time with political cartoons due to the need to draw upon wide background knowledge and complex cognitive strategies. Using the procedure outlined in the previous paragraph gives students a chance to integrate, through a graphic representation, what they understand and then to make a point about that understanding. Once students have developed an initial interest in the topic because they have drawn it, they are often more willing to find out more about the topic and create more complex cartoons based on their new knowledge. Again, as John Little has pointed out, the more students work with current events and political cartoons, the more they are willing to do so and to like doing so.

A FUNNY THING HAPPENED

To teachers, all this means carefully scaffolding the use of political cartoons while preserving the initial impact a cartoon can have. Just one cartoon isn't enough, and not just any cartoon will do. Consider the cartoon selection questions discussed earlier. The place to start, as suggested by question one, is to ensure that the cartoon fits with the standards and curriculum. How effective a cartoon will be is determined in part by the answers to questions two (Is the cartoon immediately or potentially relevant to the students?) and three (Do students have the background knowledge to understand the cartoon?). While students bring their own meaning to any reading of a selected cartoon, the teacher can give some consideration to what students might need to know and what might be relevant, or potentially so, for the students who must engage with it.

Just as important, the political cartoon is a window to a world that encourages public dialogue and respects the views of others rather than using ideology to shut out the portions of the world whose inhabitants don't see things in exactly the same way. Beyond the quick laugh of a comic strip (which is a valuable feature of comics), the political cartoon uses powerful imagery to convey ideas, evoking responses that cause viewers to challenge their own biases, look beyond those biases to a different point of view, and preserve or enlarge a perspective while allowing others the same privilege.

NOTE

1. In the days after September 11, 2001, cartoonists drew heavily on the image of the Statue of Liberty traditionally viewed by many Americans as a symbol of the national perception of the United States as a country that welcomes immigrants. Most of the images captured a weeping statue; there were over two hundred of these images. When five or more cartoonists draw virtually the same image at the same time, they call it a Yahtzee. When this happens, cartoonists may view it as a kind of groupthink that represents a lack of critical thought or creative approach to the topic (D. Cagle, e-mail, January 15, 2006). By illustrating the Statue of Liberty with a knife in her back, the Matson cartoon took a different stance than many cartoonists who attempted to make sense of the events on September 11, 2001.

REFERENCES

Bartlett, F. C. (1932). *Remembering: A study in experimental and social psychology.* Cambridge: Cambridge University Press.

Betts, E. A. (1946). *Foundations of reading instruction.* New York: American Book Company.

Cheyne, J. A., & Tarulli, D. (1999). Dialogue, difference, and voice in the zone of proximal development. *Theory and Psychology, 9,* 5–29.

Dechant, E. (1991). *Understanding and teaching reading: An interactive model.* Hillsdale, NJ: Lawrence Erlbaum Associates.

Fisher, D., & Wolsey, T. D. (in press). *Learning to predict and learning from predictions: How thinking about what might happen next helps students learn.* Upper Saddle River, NJ: Merrill Prentice Hall.

Gillespie, C. S. (1993). Reading graphic displays: What teachers should know. *Journal of Reading, 36,* 350–354.

Justice, B. (2005). Thomas Nast and the public school of the 1870s. *History of Education Quarterly, 45*(2), 171–206.

Kirkeby, C. (2005). Current events project #5. Retrieved January 13, 2006, from http://www.cagle.com/teacher/5.asp

Kolb, D. A. (1984). *Experiential learning: Experience as a Source of Learning.* Englewood Cliffs, NJ: Prentice Hall.

Lamb, C. (2004). *Drawn to extremes: The use and abuse of editorial cartoons.* New York: Columbia University Press.

McConnell, S. (1992). Talking drawings: A strategy for assisting learners. *Journal of Reading, 36,* 260–269.

National Center for Education Statistics. (2001). *Highlights of U.S. Results from the International IEA Civic Education Study (CivEd).* Retrieved December 30, 2005, from: http://nces.ed.gov/pubs2001/cived/index.asp

Rakes, G. C. (1999). Teaching visual literacy in a multimedia age. *TechTrends, 43*(4), 14–18.

Reinking, D. (1988). Integrating graphic aids into content area instruction: The graphic information lesson. *Journal of Reading, 30,* 146–151.

Ryder, R. J., & Graves, M. F. (2003). *Reading and learning in the content areas,* (3rd ed.). New York: John Wiley and Sons.

Rulli, D. F. (2003). Big and famous not always best: Guidelines for selecting teachable documents. *Social Education, 67*(7), 378–380.

Tally, B., & Goldenberg, L. B. (2005). Fostering historical thinking with digitized primary sources. *Journal of Research on Technology in Education, 38*(1), 1–21.

Tharp, R. G., & Gallimore, R. (1989, Summer). Rousing schools to life. *American Educator, 13*(2), 20–25, 46–52.

Wink, J. (2005). *Critical pedagogy: Notes from the real world.* Boston: Pearson Education.

Zinn, H. (1999). *A people's history of the United States, 1492–present, twentieth anniversary edition.* New York: HarperCollins.

Cartoons

Cagle, D. (2001, October 19). How to draw a cartoon. *Cagle.com*

Cagle, D. (2002, September 9). 9/11 commercialization. *Cagle.com*

Cagle, D. (2005, July 30). Elderly space shuttle. *Cagle.com*

Matson, R. J. (2001, September 11). [Liberty knife in back]. *The New York Observer and Roll Call.*

Nast, T. (1885, April 11). [Our Ulysses: April 9, 1865—A never forgotten deed]. *Harper's Weekly.*

7

Learning From Illustrations in Picturebooks

Lawrence R. Sipe

How do very young children understand the visual literacy of their picturebooks? Sipe analyzes the elements of picturebooks and invites readers to consider the sophistication and potential of this literary form.

In this chapter, I address the aspects of visual literacy that can be learned from picture storybooks, a form of literature that can be found in virtually every primary classroom. I also argue that picturebooks are valuable resources for developing visual aesthetic understanding in all grades, including middle school and secondary school. The chapter has three main divisions. First, I define picturebooks, and describe the aspects of this special literary format, "touring" picturebooks, as it were, in an effort to share useful information about their special qualities. Second, I describe how the visual information in picturebooks can be interpreted by students, using examples from my own research. Last, I consider what educational practitioners can do to make pedagogical use of all this information.

WHAT ARE PICTUREBOOKS LIKE?

Most educators in the United States are familiar with books like Maurice Sendak's (1963) *Where the Wild Things Are,* often considered the quintessential picturebook, and *The Polar Express* (Van Allsburg, 1985). The first thing you will notice about such books is their brevity: Generally, a picturebook is only 32 pages long. Occasionally, as in *Where the Wild Things Are,* the number is extended to 40 (or more)—always multiples of 8 because of the way the pages are printed on both sides of large sheets of paper and then cut, folded, and bound. Not only does the entire book comprise a limited number of pages; as well, there is often a rather small amount of text for each page, so that the illustrations, which occur on virtually every page, take up a great deal of space. The overall impression, then, is that of a book with a great number of pictures and with correspondingly few words compared to a novel or a "chapter book." For example, the entire text of *Where the Wild Things Are* has 338 words, whereas, from the beginning of this chapter to the end of the sentence you are reading now, you will have already reached approximately the same amount of words. Thus, the relatively high proportion of space devoted to visual information (like illustrations) and the relatively low proportion of space devoted to the words of the story are two of the defining features of picturebooks. Indeed, some picturebooks are wordless, or nearly so.

But it is not only the small number of words and large number of pictures that define picturebooks; even more crucial is the *relationship* of the words and pictures. In a picturebook, the pictures (and other visual information) are absolutely necessary—as necessary as the words, or even more so—in telling the story. The words of *Where the Wild Things Are,* alone, would be incomplete and confusing without the pictures; with no illustrations, the book would cease to exist. On the other hand, a text like *The Secret Garden* (Burnett, 1911/1984) stands alone. We can imagine an expensive, profusely illustrated edition of this story, with lovely pictures on every page (though it would be a very long book indeed). However, none of these visual images would be crucial to our understanding and appreciation of the story. This is why *picturebooks* must be distinguished from *illustrated* books. It is also why the relationship between the words and pictures is so important.

Our society and our schools are both word-centered; and, although with the advent of television, cinema, and the Internet, this dominance seems to be weakening, we still tend to privilege words over pictures. With a picturebook, this must not be the case, because the words and pictures work together on an equal footing to produce a total effect. In the words of author-illustrator Mini Grey (2006), "When people talk about illustrations in books, it often sounds like the words are in charge and the pictures are just following orders. But I think that in picture books it's different. In picture books, words and pictures are a fantastic double act, each doing a different job, maybe even telling a different story—but you need both of them to have the whole story" (p. 20). Here, Grey uses the two-word term "picture book," whereas I (along with a number of other theorists and practitioners, such as Barbara Kiefer, David Lewis, Maria Nikolajeva, Carole Scott, Evelyn Arizpe, and Morag Styles) use the compound word "picturebook" to emphasize the inextricable connection of words and pictures and the unique qualities of the form: a picturebook is not simply a book that happens to have pictures. Grey also uses a theatrical metaphor—a "double act"—in describing the relationships of words and pictures in picturebooks. Others have employed musical metaphors, such as the words and pictures comprising a "duet" (Cech, 1983–1984), or images evoking textiles; Moss (1990, p. 21) writes of the "interweaving of text and pictures." I use the word "synergy" (Sipe, 1998a), arguing that the text and pictures produce a whole that is greater together than the sum of the individual parts.

Grey has made the point that words and pictures can have a variety of relationships in picturebooks. They can each do a "different job," or tell different stories. Nodelman (1988) suggests that words and pictures never tell exactly the same story, and are frequently in an ironic relationship with one another. For example, when Max meets the Wild Things, the text relates that "they roared their terrible roars and gnashed their terrible teeth and rolled their terrible eyes and showed their terrible claws"—pretty scary! However, the pictures don't match the words: the Wild Things are rather amusing, pudgy characters, more like stuffed animals than frightening monsters. So the words and pictures, in this case, are in an ironic relationship with one another. Nodelman also suggests that words "limit" the pictures while the pictures also "limit" the words. To use another example from *Wild Things*, at the beginning of the story, Max is pictured wearing a white outfit with a bushy tail, buttons, whiskers, and ears, while banging a nail into the wall to construct a makeshift tent. The accompanying text reads, "The night Max wore his wolf suit and made mischief of one kind . . . " Here, the picture limits the words, by describing just what kind of "mischief" Max is perpetrating and what, exactly, his "wolf suit" looks like. Correspondingly, the words limit the picture by telling us that all this happened at night and that the human figure is a boy named Max (the gender of the figure in the illustration is ambiguous). The words also limit the picture by telling us what visual details we should pay attention to out of the great array of possibilities. So the words tell us things that the pictures omit, and the pictures tell us things about which the words are silent: in a well-made picturebook, neither the words nor the pictures could tell the story alone. Thus, there are a number of complex ways in which the words and pictures in picturebooks may interrelate. Nikolajeva and Scott (2001) suggest that there are at least five relationships: (1) "symmetry" or virtual equivalence between words and pictures; (2) "complementarity" (words and pictures each contribute information to one story);

(3) "enhancement," where words and pictures extend each other's meaning; (4) "counterpoint"—words and pictures tell different stories; and (5) "contradiction," in which the words and pictures flatly contradict each other.

An important implication of these various text-picture relationships is that, as readers/viewers, we must always interpret the words in terms of the pictures and the pictures in terms of the words, in an intricate and recursive process some call "transmediation" (Suhor, 1984; Sipe, 1998a). This continual back-and-forth "relaying" (Barthes, 1978) between text and pictures means that the best and most fruitful readings of picturebooks are never straightforwardly linear, but rather involve a lot of rereading, turning to previous pages, reviewing, slowing down, and reinterpreting. Doonan (1993) suggests that there is an inherent tension in picturebooks: the words impel us forward to find out what happens, whereas the pictures invite us to savor and linger. All of this has important consequences for how educators use these books in classrooms. Children (and teachers) need time to examine and carefully interpret the ways in which words and pictures relate to each other in these types of books.

One final important aspect of picturebooks: Navigating them requires that we pay attention to every feature, from the front cover and the dust jacket to the back cover. We can't just skip to the first words of the story and begin reading; if we do, it's like arriving at the opera after the overture is finished (Moebius, 1986). Instead, we should carefully study both the words and pictures on the front and back covers to give us an idea of what the story will be like. We should remove the dust jacket (if there is one) to see if perhaps the inside board cover is different from the dust jacket (the books of illustrator Jan Brett are famous for creating this surprise). We should speculate on why the illustrator, designer, or editor made this choice, communicating to children that every single detail of the book—down to the typefaces, the size and shape of the book, and the placement of the illustrations on the pages—is the result of somebody's decision.

As we open a picturebook, the first thing we see is the endpapers (sometimes called end pages). Here there is much visual information to interpret. Are the front endpapers identical to the back endpapers, or are they different in subtle or dramatic ways? Why? What do the visual images or the choice of color tell us about the book we are examining? Even a plain colored endpaper is the result of a decision; why, for example, are the end pages of James Marshall's (1987) version of *Red Riding Hood* green, rather than the more predictable red? Could it be that Marshall is having a little joke, since we are expecting red and get its complement on the color wheel? Or because the main action takes place in a leafy forest? We should encourage such speculations by the children; this helps to develop their critical thinking, inference-making ability, and visual interpretation skills.

When we leave the endpapers, we encounter either the half-title page (with only the title of the book and perhaps an illustration) or the title page (with the full publishing information). What can these pages tell us? What about the dedication page, or the page with the "front matter," with its copyright, ISBN information, and so on? It is only after examining all of these pages (as in listening to the overture of the opera), that we are ready to actually begin reading the words of the story. And, like the overture, this experience will have prepared us for the story in a number of ways. We will have some predictions about what the story will be about; we will also have a sense of the general tone or mood of the story—serious or light-hearted, sad or joyful. We will possibly have been introduced to setting, the literary genre to which the story belongs, and the main characters, and we may know something about their interrelationships. As we read the story, we can confirm or disconfirm these predictions and expectations. Similarly, at the end of the story, we have the back endpapers to examine, as well as the back cover. In other words, I am arguing that—literally from cover to cover—the picturebook is an art object, an aesthetic whole; that is, every one of its parts contributes to the total effect, and therefore every part is worthy of study and interpretation.

INTERPRETING VISUAL INFORMATION IN PICTUREBOOKS WITH STUDENTS

How do all these aspects of the picturebook play out in the hands of a skillful teacher with a classroom of children? This section describes just a few of the surprisingly sophisticated and insightful instances of meaning-making that even young children can display when they are encouraged and taught to look at picturebooks with care and thought. Although the examples are based on my research with primary-grade children, they point to the great potential of using picturebooks with all ages.

Children's "Reading" of Visual Signs

Particular colors can have meaningful associations in our culture. For example, red is often associated with excitement, anger, or drama, whereas blue is associated with calm, peace, and coolness. Molly Bang's (1999) *When Sophie Gets Angry—Really, Really Angry* uses both of these conventional associations. At the beginning of the story, Sophie becomes excited and angry when she has a dispute with her sister about a toy. As she calms down, the predominant colors in the illustrations change from red-orange to blue and green. First-graders noticed this change: they commented that "You can tell that she's calming down, because the colors are not as hot."

Another interpretation of the significance of color occurred during the reading of Christopher Coady's (1991) sinister version of *Red Riding Hood*, which ends abruptly and shockingly with the death of Red Riding Hood. In this version of the story, no woodsman comes to save either the little girl or her grandmother. Coady's illustrations are correspondingly dark and foreboding. The title page of this book contains an oval illustration of a bare tree, in front of a full moon. The tree branches and the lower border of the illustration are tinged with red. The following is a portion of the discussion about this page:

Sean: At first, there's some red strokes over the moon [pointing to the illustration of the tree branches silhouetted by the moon]

Teacher: Some red strokes over the moon.

Sean: And down there, too [pointing to the bottom curve of the illustration]

Teacher: Yes, red strokes over the moon, and over the picture here, red strokes of paint.

Nicole: Because it's Red Riding Hood.

Mickey: Because when, um, the hunter cuts him open, there's blood in the story.

Teacher: Do you think that might be something we call foreshadowing, to let you know? Foreshadowing is what allows you to predict what might happen. Because when the illustrator and the author give you little clues to foreshadow what will happen next, and to let you know what will happen next.

Julie: It is October because the leaves are not on the tree.

Teacher: And look at that moon: a full moon.

Charles: It's a warning of blood from the wolf that's going to eat the grandma.

In this vignette, Sean notices the red strokes over the moon and along the border of the illustrations, and Nicole suggests that red is appropriate for Red Riding Hood. Mickey, already knowing at least one version of the story, connects the red to blood. The teacher perceives the opportunity for a brief "teachable moment" (Eeds & Wells, 1989) to explain the concept of foreshadowing; thus these first-graders had their first introduction to this literary concept, which they were able to use for themselves later on in the school year. Julie remarks that it must be autumn, and the teacher adds reference to the moon. Then Charles sums it all up: "It's a warning of blood . . ." The discussion shows that the children are learning how to "read" the visual metaphors in the illustration. In this story, red suggests danger, warning, and blood. The association with blood in Coady's version of *Red Riding Hood* continued throughout the discussion of the book. The children built this association as they commented that there's "more and more red" in the illustrations as the story progressed. By the end of the story, the association was so strong that their response to the last illustration, which shows the empty rumpled bed with a red bedspread, was one of horror: "Look at the bed! It's full of blood!" After the story was completed, the children discussed other ways in which the illustrator had achieved the effect of "scariness." They pointed out that the illustrations are quite dark in tone, and seem to become darker as the story progresses. The teacher pointed out the odd perspectives Coady had chosen to use: in some cases, the whole picture seems slanted sharply to one side, and in other cases, the scene looms above the reader, who seems to be positioned almost on the floor or the ground. She suggested that these strange points of view reminded her of a "fun house, a scary fun house." One child compared the illustrations to "The Twilight Zone," surely one of the most disturbing and frightening television programs he had seen. Thus, the visual information—particularly the liberal use of red paint as well as the odd perspectives in many of the illustrations—helped the children to discuss the overall tone and mood of the story.

Using the Peritext

"Peritext" (Genette, 1997; Higonnet, 1990) is a term often used for all the parts of the picturebook (discussed above) that do not include the words of the story and the accompanying illustrations—the front and back covers, the endpapers, title page, dedication page, and so on. Following are some examples of first- and second-graders' use of some of these picturebook features to make meaning.

During the reading of *The Three Little Pigs* (Marshall, 1989), the teacher showed and read the front cover, which depicts the three pigs on a stage, flanked by brick-red curtains. She then opened the book and silently showed the endpapers, which have no decoration other than their brick-red color (note that in this classroom, the term "end pages" was used instead of "endpapers"). Brad commented, "Well, it's like a curtain, like on the front cover; the curtain's open, the curtain's red, and um, then the end pages, they're red, too, and it's like, like the curtain's closed, and you're getting ready for the play to start." Brad did not take these plain endpapers for granted. He used his knowledge of what a theater looks like before a play begins, and linked this to the two visual experiences of the front cover and the endpapers. Brad's interpretation was confirmed as a possibility after the reading of the book was completed and the teacher showed the class the back cover, which depicts a rear view of the pigs, onstage again, taking their bows. Brad's comment was all the more intriguing to me because, just a few months before in a doctoral seminar on picturebooks, I had heard the illustrator Will Hillenbrand say that he thought of the endpapers as the stage curtains, which appear before the play begins, and close after the play is finished. A first-grader had echoed this sophisticated concept.

Discussion of endpapers also seems to enable the understanding of structure and form in stories. After the reading of *The Napping House* (Wood, 1984), Kristin pointed out that, unlike most picturebooks, the front endpapers were different from the back endpapers. In fact, the front endpapers of this book (a dark blue-gray) contrast markedly with the back endpapers, which are azure blue. The story begins in a quiet dark house, where "everyone is sleeping." More and more humans and animals are described sleeping in the bed until a small flea awakens everyone, and the day begins. The following discussion ensued:

Sally: That makes sense, because it's dark when the story starts, so there's a darker end page, and it's lighter when the story ends. So the end page is light, back there.

Gordon: Yeah, that makes sense! Darker, then lighter. That's different, like most books, the end pages're the same on the front and the back.

In this vignette, Sally and Gordon made structural comments about the story based on the information provided by the endpapers. The overall movement of the story from everyone sleeping in the dark to everyone awakening as the day begins was described by the children.

Some picturebooks use the endpapers to begin the narrative. In Steven Kellogg's (1991) version of *Jack and the Beanstalk,* for example, the front endpapers show the giant (having descended from his sky-castle in a tornado) stealing gold, the singing harp, and the hen that lays the golden eggs from a pirate ship. The title page continues the story, depicting the giant's return to his castle via tornado; the sinking pirate ship; and our first sight of Jack, who is looking at a procession of a king and queen on horseback. On the dedication page, Jack is shown offering a bunch of flowers to the daughter of the king and queen; this is the princess he will marry at the end of the story. Thus, the peritext of this book supplies a great deal of background information and preliminary narrative before the verbal text begins. All of these details were noted by the children. Robert noticed that "the story shows how the giant got the gold." Don said, "First the giant steals the gold from the pirates, and then, Jack steals the gold from the giant."

Also present on the end pages, title page, and dedication page of Kellogg's *Jack and the Beanstalk* are images of a hot-air balloon with a bearded man in a star-studded robe. This man is also depicted on the first and second openings. On the first opening (the beginning of the verbal text), the man holds a book in which he is painting. The arrangement of golden blocks on this small book is identical with the arrangement of the large golden text blocks on the opened book we hold in our hands. The implication is that this wizard is writing the story—the very story we are reading. On the second opening, the wizard is depicted as the one who sells the magical beans to Jack. It was not until the teacher had completed reading the story that Don discovered the meaning of this figure and its part in the story:

Hey, that guy is writing the book! This [pointing to the golden rectangular block on the left-hand page of the book the wizard is holding] is this [pointing to the rectangular block on the left-hand page of the book itself]. And this [pointing to the square block on the right-hand page of the book the wizard is holding] is this [pointing to the square block on the right-hand page of the book itself]! He's probably an artist, maybe a magician, too!

Don then turned to the end of the book, pointing out that the wizard was also depicted on the back end pages: "He's here again at the end. And the book says "finished." [The small book the wizard is holding has the word "finis".] He made the book. He's the magician, the guy who made the whole entire book!" Then he made another discovery. Excitedly turning to the second opening, Don pointed out the wizard again, commenting, "Hey, he's *also* the guy who sold the beans to Jack!" Don's series of discoveries demonstrates the potential of the peritext in refining and extending the children's understanding about the narrative. It also demonstrates the way in which illustrations alone can carry the story line, as well as children's understanding of this concept.

Understanding Storybook Characters From Illustrations

Children can learn to use illustrations to make important inferences about storybook characters. Character appearance, of course, is immediately apparent in illustrations. What characters wear; how tall or short they are; and what their visual features are like are all elements to notice and discuss. Why, for example, does the pig who builds the house of bricks in James Marshall's (1989) *The Three Little Pigs* wear a business suit, whereas his brothers dress much more shabbily and informally? As one kindergarten child put it, "He's the smart one—so he's wearing better clothes!" During a reading of *Swamp Angel* (Isaacs, 1994), first-graders discussed the main character's size. In this tall tale, the heroine is literally larger than life. The art on the cover of the book shows a man and a woman at the bottom of the page looking upward; looming above them is a gigantic young woman, bending over to fit within the confines of the illustration frame. Her upper back and the top of her head are not visible; in other words, her body "breaks the frame" of the illustration. Children commented:

Charles: She's too big for the picture!

Julie: She's bent over; she's trying to get out!

Teacher: This is one way the illustrator shows that this girl is very, very tall.

Children can also use illustrations to describe characters' actions or movements. For example, during the reading of Jon Scieszka's (1989) *The*

True Story of the Three Little Pigs, the children delightedly observed that the ingredients for the cake the wolf makes for his "dear old granny" contains some unusual materials:

Mary: He's cooking bunny ears!

In a later illustration, they also described the pig with his razor:

Steven: He's shaving. But he forgot the shaving cream!

Characters' feelings, thoughts, dispositions, and personalities are also depicted in illustrations. For example, the back cover of Steven Kellogg's (1997) *The Three Little Pigs* shows a reformed and chastened wolf standing on a beach, wearing a shirt with the words "Thugs need hugs, too." His arms are outstretched toward several pigs, who look anxious and concerned. Children commented on this illustration, interpreting the wolf's change of heart from a bad guy to a good guy:

Melanie: He's like, "Hey Piggy!" on the back right here. "I'm not bad at all."

Dominique: 'Cuz he's nice.

Rob: He's nice *now.*

A character's clothing or hairstyle can also help children to interpret his or her personality and can also assist in creating an emotional bond between the character and the readers of the story. For example, David Delamare's (1993) version of *Cinderella* contains an illustration of several dancing couples at the ball. In this illustration, Cinderella is at the forefront, and is the only character looking directly at the viewer. The other characters sport elaborate, mannered hairstyles, in the formal style of the eighteenth century. By contrast, Cinderella has a simple, more natural hairstyle. As well, Cinderella's ball gown is understated and elegant in its simplicity, whereas the other women—including her stepsisters—wear gowns with garish colors and bold patterns. This choice of clothing and hairstyle suggests both Cinderella's purity and the vulgar qualities of her stepsisters. Children noticed these differences:

Tony: Why do they all have funky hair except Cinderella?

Teacher: Yes, I wonder.

Katie: Probably the illustrator wants me to like Cinderella—and the other people look stupid.

Thus, the children understood that the illustrator creates a bond between them and Cinderella: Her hair and clothing look much more familiar and contemporary. In contrast, the strange hairstyles and clothing of the stepsisters result in emotional distance from the children.

The physical grouping of characters in illustrations also provides clues about how they relate to each other. For example, in the opening images of *The Tale of Peter Rabbit* (1902/1991), Beatrix Potter portrays Mother Rabbit, Flopsy, Mopsy, and Cotton-tail clustered together in a solid mass. Peter, however, faces away from the rest of his family, and stands apart from them. Thus he is portrayed as literally "turning away" from his mother and sisters, which foreshadows his disobedience in the story—he will shortly turn away from the task of gathering blackberries in order to sneak into Mr. McGregor's garden. First-graders noticed this:

Nancy: Peter's turning away—he's already thinking about getting into trouble.

Teacher: He's not paying attention to his mother like Flopsy, Mopsy, and Cotton-tail, is he?

Here, the teacher affirms Nancy's inference, which places Peter outside the obedient circle of his sisters.

Visual Analysis of Artistic Media

With a teacher's encouragement, students can become fascinated with the artistic medium or media that are used to create illustrations in picturebooks. We are fortunate to live in an age where printing and reproduction technologies have advanced to the extent that virtually any piece of art can be reproduced in a picturebook; this increases the possibilities for illustrators' use of different types of media, from traditional watercolor and acrylic paint to pastels, batik, collages of mixed media, and a multitude of other techniques. Many contemporary picturebooks contain a note about the media that were used to create the illustrations. "How do you think this illustration was made?" is a question that invites speculation and further learning. One example of a teacher's use of this rich potential occurred in a combination first- and second-grade classroom. Krissy, a particularly artistic and sensitive child, became intrigued with the watercolor technique of Jerry Pinkney. She studied illustrations by Pinkney in several books, and became quite an expert at describing his flowing style, with its dappled light and shadow. The classroom teacher and I decided to further Krissy's interest by comparing Pinkney's style with the shimmering light-filled images of Impressionist paintings, particularly by Monet and Seurat. Krissy studied reproductions of work by these painters and shared her enthusiasm for this beautiful style with her classmates. Children seemed particularly drawn to the work of Seurat, with its use of thousands of dots or spots of bright color in order to produce a glittering effect of the play of light over surfaces of landscapes. This interest bore fruit later on in the school year, during the teacher's readaloud of *The Sweetest Fig* (Van Allsburg, 1993). The illustrations in this book can best be described as "grainy" or "granular"; it appears as if they were photographed through a delicate screen. Mickey, another student, noticed this, and commented, "Hey, that looks like that guy with the dots! What's his name—Seurat?" What had begun as Krissy's fascination with the dappled watercolor style of Jerry Pinkney had ended in Mickey's ability to see the similarities between Chris Van Allsburg's art in *The Sweetest Fig* and the work of Seurat. These first- and second-graders were well on their way to visual aesthetic understanding and enjoyment because they had learned to look closely at picturebooks.

WHAT EDUCATORS CAN DO TO DEVELOP CHILDREN'S VISUAL INTERPRETATION SKILLS

This chapter has touched on only a few of the potentials for visual interpretation in picturebooks, but perhaps it has given you a sense of what is possible, as well as a sense of the payoffs for students in terms of higher-level critical thinking, inference-making, and literary understanding. I think that, in general, the most important thing educators can do to develop children's visual literacy is to adopt an inquiring stance themselves in relation to picturebooks. The best preparation for reading a picturebook with students is for you to know it well—to have thought carefully about the illustrations' content and form, about how the words and pictures relate to one another, and about the ways in which the picturebook, from cover to cover, represents a unified artistic whole. Furthermore, I would *trust the book itself* to be its own best introduction; in other words, I don't advocate that you prepare many "purpose-setting" questions beforehand, or conduct so-called "picture walks" through the book in order to "get children ready." Whatever else they do, an abundance of purpose-setting questions establishes one thing: that you as the teacher are in charge, and that you have a definite "agenda." In a way, this immediately cuts children off from the speculative, hypothesizing stance we want to encourage in order to promote their visual interpretive abilities. As well, picture walks contradict the basic premise that a double-page spread of illustrations is meant to be viewed *at the same time* as the words on that spread are read, as well as the idea that the words and pictures work with each other to create a coherent experience. Thus, picture walks contradict the foundational principles of picturebooks, and can spoil the anticipation and surprise that is part of the pleasure of reading picturebooks. By trusting the book itself to be its own best introduction, then, I mean that thorough discussion of the visual and verbal information on the front and back covers, end pages, title page, and dedication pages is the best preparation for understanding and interpreting the book.

Though there is no one best way to read picturebooks with students, I do advocate an interactive approach to reading aloud (Barrentine, 1996) because I have found that it elicits imaginative, rich, and critically sophisticated interpretations from students. This means pausing after the reading of each page for children's comments and questions, rather than immediately asking your own questions. It means following the children's lead in many cases: valuing what they say, connecting one child's comment with another's, and probing children's responses to encourage them to think more deeply and critically. Interactive readalouds are not free-for-alls; teachers control the discussion, but not to the degree that the experience becomes what Eeds and Wells (1989) call a "gentle inquisition" about the story; rather our goal is to have "grand conversations" with children—what Barnes (1992) calls "exploratory talk" rather than "final draft" talk. Teachers should rarely ask questions to which they already know the answer—these are really pseudo-questions, more suited to testing than to teaching. Open-ended questions that encourage inference and multiple possible answers are the key. Interactive readalouds also presuppose that there is no set agenda other than the desire to explore a picturebook seriously with children. This does not mean that, for example, a thematic study of "friendship" shouldn't include a reading of *Amos & Boris* (Steig, 1971). However, to read *Amos & Boris* solely as a didactic way of talking about friendship is to ignore this book as a piece of literary and visual art (Allen et al., 1995).

Teachers should consider what roles they themselves play in reading picturebooks with children. In my own research with teachers who seemed to be quite successful in developing children's visual aesthetic abilities (Sipe, 2000; Sipe & Bauer, 2001), I found at least five roles. As *readers* of the text, teachers interpret and enact stories, giving voice to the silent words on the page. They divide the story into segments as they read. They act as tour guides or docents for the book by drawing children's attention to certain features ("here are the end pages"). As *managers and encouragers*, teachers praise children for their insights and create an atmosphere of responsiveness and comfort that supports the children in taking risks; as well, they model the ways in which discussion can proceed in an orderly way that encourages everyone to respond and listen to one another. As *clarifiers and probers*, teachers push children to articulate their responses more fully and to explain their thoughts to their classmates, in order to clarify their thinking and to reach higher levels of interpretation and understanding. As *fellow wonderers and speculators*, teachers place themselves in the position of fellow students, yielding some of their power and control. For example, teachers who say, "I'm not sure, either; what do you think?" empower students to think for themselves rather than relying on the teacher for answers to puzzling aspects of the story. Tolerance of ambiguity and multiple interpretations will result in higher levels of thinking. Asking questions that begin "Why do you suppose . . . ?" is a good way to gently join the conversation without dominating it. For example, "Why do you suppose that James Marshall chose to have green endpapers for *Red Riding Hood?*" Notice that this is a real question, a question to which the teacher doesn't know the answer, and that it can have many plausible answers. Finally, teachers act as *extenders and refiners* by introducing new terms and concepts as they perceive what Eeds and Wells (1989) call "teachable moments" in the conversation. These teachable moments can be quite brief, yet they are very powerful. You will remember the teacher's insertion of a teachable moment about the concept of foreshadowing in the discussion of the Coady version of *Red Riding Hood,* mentioned above; this took about fifteen seconds, but was introduced in a powerful context, and that made it memorable for the children. My advice is to tape record one of your readalouds of a picturebook, and then listen to the tape, noting how many of these roles you play, and roughly calculate the proportion of your talk that is devoted to each. In this way, you can determine what additional roles you might add to your repertoire and how you might diversify your scaffolding of the children's talk. Clearly, discussing picturebooks with students is an art that improves with practice.

Teachers should pay attention to the "page breaks" in picturebooks. Picturebooks are carefully designed as a series of double-page spreads. Between one double-page spread and the next, there is a pause, and a gap, as we turn the page. This is in contrast to a film, where there is continuous action. It also contrasts with a novel, where the page breaks are arbitrary, whereas in a picturebook, each page break has been carefully planned. Therefore, what happens between one spread and the next is a rich site for interpretation. Consider, for example, the second spread of *Where the Wild Things Are,* where Max is shown with an evil glint in his eye, chasing the family dog with a fork. The next spread shows him in his bedroom with a defiant frown on his face. What happens *between* these two spreads? The text tell us only partially: "his mother called him 'WILD THING!' and Max said 'I'LL EAT YOU UP!' so he was sent to bed without eating anything." Children could speculate that Mother has seen Max chasing the dog, and has discovered the hole in the wall made by the nail. She might have said, "All right, buddy, that's enough—what in the world are you doing? That poor dog didn't do anything to you, and you're scaring it to death! 'I'LL EAT YOU UP,' huh? Well, buster, I have news for you—I'm marching you straight to your room, and you won't eat *me* up—in fact, you won't be eating *anything* for a while!" The point here is to let children fill in the gaps represented by the page breaks with imagined dialogue and action.

One of the best ways of increasing children's visual interpretive skills is to read a series of versions or variants of the same story, each with different illustrations. For example, I read five variants of the Rapunzel story to a combined first- and second-grade class (Sipe, 2001a). I chose Rapunzel because few children knew the story; therefore, most of them were starting from a very small prior knowledge base. Thus I could trace how they developed an ever-increasingly sophisticated understanding of this story as they heard each successive variant. From the second variant onward, they made many interesting connections to the previous versions, critically comparing and contrasting the illustrations' details, styles, and moods. They also spoke about what each illustrator chose to highlight, and what each chose to omit.

Another variant of this "text set" technique (Harste, Short, & Burke, 1988) is to read a number of picturebooks illustrated by the same artist, preferably one who has a distinct and consistent style. Tomie dePaola, for example, illustrates almost all his books with a very predictable style. After viewing a number of these books, children will be able to immediately identify dePaola as the illustrator of a book that is new to them. At this point, teachers can begin to talk with children about how they were able to recognize this artist's work. What commonalities are there? There is an outline style in all of dePaola's work; figures are outlined in dark brown or black and filled in with flat areas of color with little shading. The colors are rarely brilliant or saturated; rather, there are lots of pastels. Clouds are rendered in a certain way—puffy and white. The illustrations often contain birds or religious symbols such as icons or crosses. Characters' facial expressions are depicted simply with just a few lines. Most of the illustrations are done with acrylic or watercolor washes. After you have discussed dePaola's style with the students, then choose another artist with an entirely different style, and contrast them. For example, Jerry Pinkney's work is an excellent foil. As I described above, his accomplished watercolors seem to flow loosely (there is no outlining) and have a dappled, rippling effect. The human figures, animals, and elements of landscapes appear much more realistic than dePaola's depictions. In contrast to dePaola, Pinkney is much more interested in the play of light and shadow, and his illustrations are frequently more "moody." Pinkney's pencil drawing (or "underdrawing") is often visible through the watercolor washes. Pinkney's style is also consistent across many of his books, and thus his characteristic techniques can be explored extensively. The concept of an artist's style is very complex, and needs to be built up gradually, with observations about common features across many illustrations; it's an example of building up knowledge *across cases*, in an inductive way. The pedagogical implication is that the more cases children have had to consider, the more refined and astute their understanding of style will be.

After you have done a bit of visual interpretive work with students, you might consider a group project in which students design a picturebook, complete with verbal text and matching pictures, a front and back cover, end pages, and so on. There is no better way to make students aware of all the artistic choices that have to be made when planning and executing a picturebook than to try it for themselves. A project I did with second-graders (after we experimented with many artistic media and techniques) demonstrates that this type of project can be successful even with quite young children (Sipe, 1995).

I want to emphasize that, although some picturebooks are more suited to younger children in terms of theme and subject matter, *any* picturebook can be studied by *any* age of student for the ways in which the illustrations and words relate to each other, the artistic media used in the artwork, and the meaning and interpretive possibilities of the illustrations. My graduate students and I have done exciting work with high school students in studying the perfection and sophistication of visual form and content in *Where the Wild Things Are,* a book clearly intended for a younger age. When approached as a serious and sophisticated visual aesthetic object, *Wild Things* was a wonderfully engaging piece of work for these older students.

My final piece of advice is to not be concerned about your possible lack of visual aesthetic training. As you enjoy picturebooks with students, you will become more sensitive to aspects of design, style, and content, and you will certainly learn *from* your students, because they will notice details and think of interpretations that never would have occurred to you. As well, there are a number of excellent resources that can aid you. Barbara Kiefer's (1995) *The Potential of Picturebooks* is probably the most approachable and comprehensive text to extend your visual knowledge and appreciation. Molly Bang's (2000) *Picture This* is a book written especially for educational practitioners who have little formal training in visual design; it is a delight to read, and describes basic principles of design you can immediately put into practice the next time you read a picturebook with students. Aliki's (1988) *How a Book Is Made,* a picturebook about the process of illustrating and publishing, is a resource you can read to your students, as you learn with them about the entire process, from having an idea to seeing the book in a store or library. Finally, my own work, particularly my articles "Learning the Language of Picturebooks" (Sipe, 1998b) and "Picturebooks as Aesthetic Objects" (Sipe, 2001b), will introduce you to more terms and concepts about picturebooks than I was able to highlight in this chapter. Plunge in, and you'll be surprised at how much you and the students learn about the visual riches of picturebooks.

REFERENCES

Aliki (1988). *How a book is made.* New York: HarperTrophy.

Allen, V. G., Freeman, E. B., Lehman, B. A., & Scharer, P. L. (1995). "Amos & Boris": A window on teachers' thinking about the use of literature in their classrooms. *The Reading Teacher, 48,* 384–390.

Bang, M. (2000). *Picture this: How pictures work.* San Francisco: Seastar Books.

Barnes, D. (1992). *From communication to curriculum.* Portsmouth, NH: Boynton/Cook.

Barrentine, S. J. (1996). Engaging with reading through interactive read-alouds. *The Reading Teacher, 50,* 36–43.

Barthes, R. (1978). *Image, music, text* (S. Heath, Trans.). New York: Hill & Wang.

Cech, J. (1983–1984). Remembering Caldecott: "The Three Jovial Huntsmen" and the art of the picturebook. *The Lion and the Unicorn, 7/8,* 110–119.

Doonan, J. (1993). *Looking at pictures in picturebooks*. Stroud, Gloucestershire: The Thimble Press.

Eeds, M., & Wells, D. (1989). Grand conversations: An exploration of meaning construction in literature study groups. *Research in the Teaching of English, 23,* 4–29.

Genette, G. (1997). *Paratexts: Thresholds of interpretation* (J. E. Lewin, Trans.). Cambridge: Cambridge University Press.

Grey, M. (2006). Acceptance speech for 2005 Boston Globe Horn Book Awards, Picturebook. *The Horn Book Magazine,* January/February, 17–20.

Harste, J., Short, K., & Burke, C. (1988). *Creating classrooms for authors.* Portsmouth, NH: Heinemann.

Higonnet, M. (1990). The playground of the peritext. *Children's Literature Association Quarterly, 15,* 47–49.

Kiefer, B. Z. (1995). *The potential of picturebooks: From visual literacy to aesthetic understanding.* Englewood Cliffs, NJ: Prentice-Hall.

Moebius, W. (1986). Introduction to picturebook codes. *Word and Image, 2,* 141–158.

Moss, E. (1990). A certain particularity: An interview with Janet and Allen Ahlberg. *Signal, 61,* 20–26.

Nikolajeva, M., & Scott, C. (2001). *How picturebooks work.* New York: Garland.

Nodelman, P. (1988). *Words about pictures: The narrative art of children's picturebooks.* Athens, GA: The University of Georgia Press.

Sipe, L. R. (1995). Connecting visual and verbal literacy: Second graders learn about art techniques in picturebooks. *Teacher Research: The Journal of Classroom Inquiry, 2,* 61–73.

Sipe, L. R. (1998a). How picturebooks work: A semiotically framed theory of text-picture relationships. *Children's Literature in Education, 29,* 97–108.

Sipe, L. R. (1998b). Learning the language of picturebooks. *Journal of Children's Literature, 24,* 66–75.

Sipe, L. R. (2000). The construction of literary understanding by first and second graders in oral response to picture storybook readalouds. *Reading Research Quarterly, 35,* 252–275.

Sipe, L. R. (2001a). A palimpsest of stories: Young children's intertextual links during readalouds of fairytale variants. *Reading Research and Instruction, 40,* 333–352.

Sipe, L. R. (2001b). Picturebooks as aesthetic objects. *Literacy Teaching and Learning: An International Journal of Early Reading and Writing, 6,* 23–42.

Sipe, L. R., & Bauer, J. T. (2001). Urban kindergartners' literary understanding of picture storybooks. *The New Advocate, 14,* 329–342.

Suhor, C. (1984). Towards a semiotics-based curriculum. *Journal of Curriculum Studies, 16,* 247–257.

Children's Books Cited

Bang, M. (1999). *When Sophie gets angry—really, really angry.* New York: Blue Sky Press.

Burnett, F. H. (1911/1984). *The secret garden.* New York: Dell Publishing Co.

Coady, C. (1991). *Red Riding Hood.* New York: Dutton Children's Books.

Delamare, D. (1993). *Cinderella.* New York: Green Tiger Press.

Isaacs, A. (1994). *Swamp angel.* New York: Dutton Children's Books.

Kellogg, S. (1991). *Jack and the beanstalk.* New York: Morrow.

Kellogg, S. (1997). *The three little pigs.* New York: Morrow.

Marshall, J. (1987). *Red Riding Hood.* New York: Dial.
Marshall, J. (1989). *The three little pigs.* New York: Dial.
Potter, B. (1902/1991). *The tale of Peter Rabbit.* London: Warne.
Scieszka, J. (1989). *The true story of the three little pigs.* New York: Viking.
Sendak, M. (1963). *Where the wild things are.* New York: HarperCollins.
Steig, W. (1971). *Amos & Boris.* New York: Farrar, Straus and Giroux.
Van Allsburg, C. (1985). *The Polar Express.* Boston: Houghton Mifflin.
Van Allsburg, C. (1993). *The sweetest fig.* Boston: Houghton Mifflin.
Wood, A. (1984). *The napping house.* San Diego: Harcourt Brace & Co.

8

An Irrecusable Offer

Film in the K–12 Classroom

Lawrence Baines

*We know film can entertain; how can it be used in the classroom? Baines
offers suggestions for using moving pictures to engage and teach.*

Pity the moviegoer who attends a film festival these days and forgets
to turn off the loud, melodic ring of his cellular telephone. At every
film festival, the standard mantra has become, "Turn off all electronic
devices. Please help us preserve the sacred space of the theater." The idea
of movie theater as "sacred space" is nothing new. As early as the sixth
century BCE, the Greeks built huge theaters to hold productions created in
honor of the gods (Anthon, 1899). Today, the theater is likely to be part of
a gigantic entertainment complex, replete with a special sound system,
huge screen, and comfortable chairs.

While some pioneers in education suggested that film could be
effectively integrated into the K–12 curriculum (Charters, 1933), others
began to decry film as intellectually vapid (Boutwell, 1952) or even
"satanic" (Neal, 1913). Over the years, few scholars (Golden, 2006) have

continued to promote film as a vehicle to foster the intellect, let alone the spirit.

Perhaps the conception of film as "pure entertainment" is evolving. Recently, I attended a seminar promoting the idea of motion pictures as "visual parables." Held in a church, the seminar was run by a retired minister who travels the country demonstrating how to use film to high-light tenets of Christian doctrine (McNulty, 2005). I was one of the few unordained persons in the audience. The retired minister showed the entirety of the film *Baghdad Café*, stopping occasionally to discuss the interplay between sin and redemption and the "Christ-like" figure of the main character, a large German woman stranded in a desert in the southwestern United States. According to the retired minister, establishing film clubs at church and integrating film into the worship service were two ways to get the congregation to begin "seeing theologically."

Ever since the premiere of the first film by the brothers Lumiere in 1895 (a not-very-exciting sequence depicting workers walking out of a factory), a small contingent of educators have advocated the use of film in teaching (Costanzo, 1985, 1992, 2004; Maynard, 1971; Miller, 1979; Selby 1978). The overwhelming majority of teachers use film, though in a very limited way (Larsson, 2001). The sequence usually goes something like this:

1. Read a book (or a few excerpts)

2. Give a test

3. Show the film version of the book over several days

In reality, showing the film adaptation of a novel is one of the least interesting, least imaginative methods of using motion pictures. Because they are available at libraries, department stores, video rental stores, mail-order enterprises, theaters, and Internet movie sites, films are easily obtainable outside of class. When a teacher shows a film over several days, it usually raises some eyebrows. Unfortunately, this skepticism may be well warranted—the potential for misuse of film is vast.

The stereotypical "bad social studies teacher" is a coach who shows films every other day in class—not for educational purposes, but so that he or she has time to plan practices and draw up plays. This is not to disparage coaches or social studies teachers (I have served in both capaci-ties in my career), but to note that the stereotype exists because using film in this manner is not uncommon. Screening a film without comment or analysis is of limited value; screening a film that has little relationship to the curriculum is educationally indefensible.

On a visit to an English classroom at an urban high school recently, I watched as juniors read three excerpts from Herman Melville's *Moby Dick*. The total time spent reading the text was less than fifteen minutes. Then, students put away their books, the teacher pushed a copy of the 1956

John Huston–directed, two-hour film *Moby Dick* into a VCR, and students silently stared at a television screen for the next two-and-a-half days. Perhaps I exaggerate—about half the class didn't stare at the screen at all because they were asleep.

Melville and his novel were never mentioned again, nor was there any discussion about screenwriter Ray Bradbury's consistently quirky interpretation of plot and character. In this case, the film *Moby Dick* served only to give the teacher a mental vacation and to give students, at least the half of the class whose eyes remained open, a small taste of a great story.

Time would seem better spent doing almost anything else. Film can be used to achieve a variety of goals useful to the English teacher, but it takes more effort and imagination to get it done than popping a videotape into a VCR. A creative teacher operating under the most meager of budgets can invigorate the curriculum and achieve startling gains in student achievement through film (Admussen, 1978; Anderson, 1992; Beckman, Austin, & Thompson, 2004; Cennamo, 1993; Gardner, 1991; Higgins, 1991; Karl, 1981; Kerber, Clemens, & Medina, 2004; Kraft, 1987; Krendl, 1986; Loewen, 1991; McDonald, 1983; Remender, 1992; Resch & Schicker, 1992; Shiring, 1990; Squires, 1990; Vetrie, 2004). However, evidence suggests that, in general, teachers use film ineffectively (Larsson, 2001).

TEACHING VOCABULARY THROUGH FILM

Because films communicate primarily through visual symbols (with sound and music providing tone), words are usually superfluous to a screenplay. Indeed, most film scripts are written at a readability level of between second and fourth grade (Baines, 1995, 1997). Few of us leave a theater and run home and look up words in the dictionary. Although screenplays may use few polysyllabic words, film can nevertheless be an innovative tool to teach vocabulary.

Lesson Idea

A fun exercise is to have students bring in ads, posters, or the DVD covers of popular films. Replace words in an ad with "target vocabulary words" of more nuance and sophistication. For example, most students need see only the altered advertisement for the film *Pretty Woman* to understand *pulchritudinous* as a synonym for *pretty* (Figure 8.1).

To ensure that students remember *pulchritudinous* for the rest of their days, play the song by Roy Orbison (featured in the film), and have two extroverted students sing it, karaoke-style, replacing every occurrence of *pretty* with *pulchritudinous* as they sing.

Figure 8.1

A blockbuster movie starring Arnold Schwarzenegger used the title *The Terminator,* a form of a familiar word, *terminate,* to signify a plot that has to do with "eliminating completely" the human race. By substituting a synonym, *extirpate,* for *terminate,* students learn a new word, one that might come to mind when political advertisements flicker across their television screens: "How I wish I could extirpate those ads!"

A related activity is to show brief clips of famous scenes from movies, perhaps the sequence in *The Godfather* when Don Corleone (Marlon Brando) says, "I'm going to make him an offer he can't refuse." Play this two-minute clip for students in its original form. Then, play the clip a second time without sound, asking a dramatic student to say the phrase, "I'm going to make him an *irrecusable* offer" aloud at the point where Corleone speaks his famous line. The idea is that students will associate *irrecusable* with "that which cannot be refused."

> ### From *The Godfather,* 1972
>
> *Johnny:*   A month ago, he bought the movie rights to this book. A best seller—and the main character, it's a guy just like me, I, uh, I wouldn't even have to act, just be myself. Oh godfather, I don't know what to do. I don't know what to do.
>
> *Corleone:*   You can act like a man. (He slaps Johnny in the face.) What's the matter with you? Is this how you turned out? A Hollywood *finochio* that cries like a woman? (He imitates Johnny's whining.) "What can I do? What can I do?" What is that nonsense? Ridiculous. You spend time with your family?
>
> *Johnny:*   Sure I do.
>
> *Corleone:*   Good. 'Cause a man who doesn't spend time with his family can never be a real man. Come here. You look terrible. I want you to eat. I want you to rest a while. And in a month from now, this Hollywood big shot's gonna give you what you want.
>
> *Johnny:*   It's too late, they start shooting in a week.
>
> *Corleone:*   I'm gonna make him an offer he can't refuse. [I'M GOING TO MAKE HIM AN IRRECUSABLE OFFER.] Now, you just go outside and enjoy yourself, and uh, forget about all this nonsense. I want you, I want you to leave it all to me.

TEACHING GRAMMAR THROUGH FILM

As a first-year teacher, I used to take pride that I "hit grammar hard" for six weeks every year. During my "gramm cram," I flooded my students with worksheets, games, and drills about predicate nominatives, subordinate conjunctions, future perfect tenses, parallel structures, gerunds, and adverbial clauses. There were two problems with gramm cram:

1. students' writing did not improve, and
2. students remembered almost nothing about grammar twenty-four seconds after the unit was over.

One of the most difficult tasks for a teacher is to teach grammar effectively. Teachers-in-the-know may nod when they hear the phrase "teach grammar in context," but actually delivering instruction that way can be challenging. One way to contextualize grammar is to show students certain film clips that contain excessive amounts of slang, jargon, or ellipsis. The task is for students to translate bits of the film script into grammatically correct, easily understandable language.

Lesson Idea

Play a film clip straight through once. Then, replay the clip and have students write out the dialogue, stopping and starting the film as necessary. Finally, have students translate the dialogue into formal (or overly formal) English. In Figure 8.2, an excerpt from *10 Things I Hate About You* (a very loose adaptation of Shakespeare's *Taming of the Shrew*) required students to translate some heavy teen speak into more formal language.

Of course, doing the inverse—having students translate formal dialogue into their own words—can be interesting and educational as well. Figure 8.3 contains such a scene from *Romeo + Juliet* (1996).

Using film to teach grammar can help students distinguish among dialect, jargon, and academic discourse. In the past, I have used the sequence from *Ghost* (1990) where Whoopi Goldberg translates Patrick Swayze's verbose warnings to his wife into more direct language to illustrate degrees of formality in language.

A teacher might consider using selected clips from films with urban locations and infused with the slang of hip-hop, such as *Hustle & Flow* (2005) or *8 Mile* (2002). However, be forewarned—many contemporary urban films have cursing and explicit references to sex, drugs, or booze, so choose clips carefully. To reach an urban adolescent audience, clips from *Where the Red Fern Grows* (1974) just will not work as effectively as more contemporary films.

TEACHING CRITICAL THINKING THROUGH FILM

An easy interdisciplinary unit combining social studies and language arts is to have students assess the authenticity of a filmed historic event. For example, after studying a historic event, such as the Battle of the Alamo, students might enjoy examining aspects of the filmed interpretations offered by directors John Wayne (1960) and John Lee Hancock (2004). The two Alamo films address the same event, but the circumstances and characterizations are radically different. While John Wayne's version promoted the defenders of the Alamo as heroes fighting against insurmountable odds and a cold-blooded, repressive regime, Hancock's version takes an approach that is simultaneously more empathetic toward the Mexican army and more cynical about the motives of the Alamo's defenders.

Lesson Idea

Begin by reading historical accounts of an event and related primary source materials. Next, show the film version of the event and compare the two. For example, in the 1960 Alamo film, William B. Travis (commander of the

Figure 8.2

From *10 Things I Hate About You* script	Formal Revision of *10 Things I Hate About You*
JOEY That's Kat Stratford. I want you to go out with her.	JOEY Observe that young woman. Her name is Kat Stratford. I want you to engage in a symbiotic, monogamous, heterosexual union with her.
PATRICK Yeah sure, Sparky.	PATRICK That seems highly improbable, my lively friend.
JOEY Look. I can't take out her sister until Kat starts dating. You see, their dad's whacked out. He's got this rule where the girls . . .	JOEY Perceive my plight: I cannot correspondingly couple with her sister until Kat is confirmed in a stable, valid unification. Appreciate that their father is neurotic. He decrees that his daughters . . .
PATRICK That's a touching story. It really is. Not my problem.	PATRICK Unfortunately your tale reeks of sentimentality. Instead of heartfelt emotion, I feel only manipulation. I refuse to participate in your stratagem.
JOEY Would you be willing to make it your problem if I provide generous compensation?	JOEY Would a fiscal motivator influence you otherwise?
PATRICK You're going to pay me to take out some chick? How much?	PATRICK You will sponsor my merger with a young lady? What will be the rate of compensation?
JOEY Twenty bucks. (Pause). Fine. Thirty.	JOEY Twenty American dollars. (Pause). I perceive that you are offended by my offer. I am willing to increase the sum to thirty dollars.
PATRICK Well, let's think about this. We go to the movies. That's 15 bucks. We get popcorn. That's 53. And she'll want Raisinettes, right? So we're looking at 75 bucks.	PATRICK This issue deserves more thorough analysis. First, we enjoy a motion picture, costing approximately 15 dollars. Second, we consume corn kernels heated until detonation. This would increase our budget to approximately 53 dollars. The young lady will most likely desire chocolate-covered raisins, colloquially referred to as Raisinettes, no? This further raises our account to 75 dollars.
JOEY This ain't a negotiation. Take it or leave it, Trailer Park.	JOEY I refuse to barter. Please accept my original offer or respectfully decline.
PATRICK 50 bucks and it's a deal, Fabio.	PATRICK Confirm a remuneration of 50 dollars and I will agree to your terms, Libertine.

Printed with permission from David Pyles.

Figure 8.3

From the film *Romeo + Juliet* (1996)	Translated into students' contemporary language
ROMEO But soft, what light through yonder window breaks? It is the East, and Juliet is the sun! Arise, fair sun, and kill the envious moon, Who is already sick and pale with grief That thou her maid art far more fair than she. Be not her maid, since she is envious. Her vestal livery is but sick and green, And none but fools do wear it. Cast it off! It is my lady. O, it is my love! O that she knew she were!	**ROMEO** Who's that at the window? Could be that babe I saw at the dance. She is hot.
JULIET Ay me!	**JULIET** Like, I am feeling a little ditzy.
ROMEO She speaks. O, speak again, bright angel!	**ROMEO** Say what?
JULIET O Romeo, Romeo!—Wherefore art thou Romeo? Deny thy father and refuse thy name. Or, if thou wilt not, be but sworn my love, And I'll no longer be a Capulet.	**JULIET** Romeo is a weird name. That dog should try a new one to salvage his rep. If he liked me enough, I might just give it up for him.
ROMEO Shall I hear more, or shall I speak at this?	**ROMEO** Yo?
JULIET 'Tis but thy name that is my enemy. Thou are thyself, though not a Montague. What's Montague? It is not hand nor foot Nor arm nor face nor any other part Belonging to a man. O, be some other name! What's in a name? That which we call a rose By any other word would smell as sweet. So Romeo would, were he not Romeo called, Retain that dear perfection which he owes Without that title. Romeo, doff thy name, And for thy name, which is no part of thee, Take all myself.	**JULIET** Your name sucks. A name don't mean nothing. A fine looking flower would still be fine looking if you called it, like, a roach or something. If Romeo could change his name, maybe we could hook up.
ROMEO I take thee at thy word! Call me but love, and I'll be new baptized. Henceforth I never will be Romeo.	**ROMEO** I know that's right. That Romeo dude has left the building. Call me whatever you feel like.

Printed with permission from Emmett Seniab.

Texans) is wounded in the chest in the final minutes of the siege. He deftly fires back at several Mexican soldiers before receiving several more bullets. After he recoils in pain, Travis draws his sword from the sheath, breaks it in two, and collapses. In the 2004 film, Travis dies from a gunshot wound to the forehead shortly after the battle begins—a more historically accurate portrayal.

Over the past few years, the death of David (Davy) Crockett has grown into a contentious debate among historians. In the 1960 film, during the siege, Crockett clutches a torch after getting shot at close range and falls into a small building filled with gunpowder and ammunition (which, if it had been around, would surely have been put to use by the Texans). This precipitates a colorful, very loud explosion, and the subsequent demise of more Mexican soldiers. In the 2004 film, Crockett actually survives the 90-minute onslaught, but is summarily executed by General Antonio Lopez de Santa Anna shortly thereafter.

The 2004 version's depiction of Crockett's death is based upon the recollections of a Mexican soldier, José Enrique de la Peña, whose manuscripts were abruptly "discovered" under mysterious circumstances in 1955. Although the ink and paper of the document seem authentic to the time period, de la Peña's account has been disputed from a variety of perspectives, beginning with his ability to identify Crockett. The defenders of the Alamo did not carry identification cards, and it is difficult to imagine that de la Peña carried a picture of Crockett around with him.

Second, even if the document were authentic and de la Peña was somehow able to identify Crockett among the throng of corpses (182 Texans, up to 1,600 Mexican soldiers), there are several other accounts of the battle written by other Mexican soldiers that contradict de la Peña's account (Center for American History, 2005). Further analysis of Crockett's death might involve investigation into when de la Peña allegedly wrote about the Alamo (almost a year later) and his subsequent imprisonment by Mexican authorities for his anti–Santa Anna politics.

I do not mean to belabor the historical details of the Alamo, but offer this event and its two celluloid interpretations as an example of the research and writing opportunities that the pairing of history and film can engender. A teacher could proceed in a similar fashion with any event (or historical novel) and its film adaptation.

TEACHING READING AND WRITING WITH FILM

Undeniably, the most vexing aspect of teaching literature (aside from getting students to read in the first place) is getting students to read effectively. At some point, even the most competent readers have difficulty with comprehension and inference. To encourage students to reread and analyze the text, I use a game called Screen Test, which works off of film, yet no film is ever shown—not even a clip. Screen Test works best when students have read a short story or novel as a class.

Lesson Idea

Play five different pieces of music. As each piece plays, students write about a scene from a book or short story for which the music could serve as a soundtrack. Allow a minute after each song is over for students to complete their thoughts.

After all the songs have played, discuss the music in the context of the novel. Pose questions about the applicability of each piece of music—especially about songs that "did not fit." Ask students to share their responses. Have students select one song that best represents the major themes of the book and offer a brief rationale for it.

Next, have students list some popular actresses and actors capable of playing characters from the book and discuss their suitability for the roles. Have students write a persuasive essay substantiating why the actors and actresses they prefer are the most compelling choices for the lead roles.

Meg Rosoff's novel *How I Live Now* describes life after the apocalypse of a nuclear war from a teenager's perspective. The screen test for *How I Live Now* might look like this:

You are a director for a film company who is going to shoot Rosoff's How I Live Now. *First, you need a soundtrack.*

  I. Choose from the following:
  - A. Ralph Vaughan Williams: Fantasia on a theme of Thomas Tallis
  - B. The Cure: "Friday, I'm in Love"
  - C. Hildegard Von Bingen: Spiritui Sancto
  - D. Chopin, Etude Op. 10. no. 12: "Revolutionary"
  - E. Nat King Cole: "Unforgettable"
  - F. Brian Jonestown Massacre: "When Jokers Attack"

For each song, choose the scene in which you'd use the music and why you think the music appropriate. Then, choose one song that best fits the book and explain why it is appropriate.

For II and III, you may choose "unknowns," but you will need to explain the physical traits, presence, and mannerisms you expect.

  II. What actresses would be perfect for the part of Daisy? Explain why you think the actress you have chosen is most appropriate.

  III. What actor would be perfect to play Edmond? Explain why you think the actor you have chosen is most appropriate.

  IV. What locations would you use to shoot the film? Why these settings?

Although students are forced to reread and reexamine portions of the text for Screen Test, they enjoy selecting the soundtrack and playing casting director. This particular exercise puts the cult of celebrity to constructive use by placing students in positions of simulated power over some of the most recognizable names in show business. A student sample of the music portion of the exercise follows:

Music for the soundtrack to
"HOW I LIVE NOW"

A. Ralph Vaughan Williams:
    Fantasia on a theme of Thomas Tallis

The part where Daisy is walking over all the dead bodies in the farmyard as she searches sadly for Piper. Then when she finds Piper crying and holding onto her goat.

B. Cure
    "Friday, I'm in Love."
This song is possibly a good representation of scenes of Daisy and Edmond as they lay outside and the cousins are swimming. Edmond's smoking and Daisy feels the warmth "pull" of his body. The war's going on but Daisy doesn't have a care in the world because she's in love.

C. Hildegard Von Bingen
    Spiritui Sancto
The "echo" and hollow sound of this piece of music makes me think of Daisy in the hospital as she feels like she's dying of loss. She's sad, lonely and feels empty.

(Continued)

(Continued)

D. Chopin, Etude Op 10. no 12
   "Revolutionary"
Daisy and her cousins as they're torn
apart and loaded into the cars
by the men with guns and hauled
away...torn emotionally and quickly
from one another, uncertain of
what's going to happen.

E. Nat King Cole,
   "Unforgettable"
   I see Daisy dreaming of her mother,
wondering intensely what she was like.
Then I see Aunt Penn coming in and
reading her mind, sitting down with Daisy
and spilling her heart and memory
out about what her sister (Daisy's mother)
was like. She'd even tell her all the
things Daisy thought would never be
answered.

F. Brian Jonestown Massacre
   "When Jokers Attack"
   I see Aunt Penn running frantically
around the train station with people
everywhere. Some hurt, some dead,
some crying, and some numb like
zombies. Then there's Penn standing
in the midst of it, tired, scared and
alone.

conclusion

   I think the best song would be Spiritui
Sancto by Hildegard Von Bingen. The
songs emptiness conveys the emtiness
and depression of Daisy which is
felt through so many scenes of the
book. Not only is it appropriate
for Daisy's hospital visit, but several
other scenes where you know the young
girl feels alone and empty, and
depressed by her life's circumstances.

Not only does Screen Test assess students' recollection of events and characters, but it helps clarify a literary work's tone, plot, and themes. In selecting actors and actresses for a film, students typically go to great lengths to advocate for a particular public figure who has caught their fancy. Because students often feel "personally invested" in the task of convincing the rest of class that their choices are appropriate, Screen Test provides an opportunity to teach the persuasive essay.

USING FILM TO ENHANCE STUDENTS' SPEAKING SKILLS

Incredibly, few teachers use cameras to record student progress over time. With the new generation of camcorders, teachers need only point and shoot to capture a moment and store it on the computer. To view the results on a large screen requires only a cord to connect to a computer. To produce a copy of a video on DVD takes two clicks.

Imagine having a DVD of yourself reading from your writing portfolio at the beginning and end of every year from kindergarten to twelfth grade. Film documents progress over time and serves as an unimpeachable archive of achievement, style, and personality. While parents, students, and administrators may quibble over grades or written comments, a film is irrefutable.

The mere presence of a camera during a class activity has a dramatic effect on student attitudes. Initially, when students see the camera, they become hyperconscious about their behavior. Suddenly, they try to fix their hair, make funny faces, wave, and act silly—but this does not last long. If students know that a film starring them will be shown to members of class, their concern level rises exponentially. A smart teacher can use such heightened attention to intensify student learning.

Teaching Idea

Filming student speeches is one of the most practical ways to get students to hone their speaking skills. Begin by showing film clips of some effective American speakers—Martin Luther King, Ronald Reagan, Barack Obama, Hillary Clinton—then ask students to identify characteristics of an effective speech. Show a film clip of a speech once without comment and ask students to identify aspects of the speech that seem particularly compelling or weak. From this, build a rubric for the assessment of an effective speech. A sample rubric for the evaluation of a speech follows:

Excellent (12 points each)	Good (10 points each)	Needs work (0–8 points each)
A. At least two appropriate citations (or quotations) from texts	A. Citations from texts are not always related to the theme of the speech	A. No citations from texts
B. At least two appropriate pieces of data	B. Data lacks development or not as strong as it could be	B. No supporting data
C. An effective anecdote	C. An anecdote that is only indirectly related	C. No anecdote
D. At least two graphics that are appropriate to the theme of the speech	D. Graphics that may lack originality or are not clearly related to the theme of the speech	D. No graphics
E. Introduction that gets the attention of the audience	E. Introduction may not be well developed	E. Flat or inappropriate introduction
F. Material is well organized.	F. Material is somewhat organized	F. Not well organized
G. Language choices are precise	G. Some language choices are precise	G. Ineffective language choices
H. Appropriate grammar and syntax for an oral speech	H. Some appropriate grammar and syntax	H. Inappropriate grammar and syntax
I. Voice is sufficiently loud and understandable	I. Voice is sometimes not loud or understandable	I. Voice is often not loud enough or is difficult to understand
J. Body language is appropriate to the message	J. Body language is sometimes inappropriate for the message	J. Body language is often at odds with the message

Filmed speeches are available through many media and Web sites, including American Rhetoric (www.americanrhetoric.com), Douglass Archives (http://douglassarchives.org/), and The History Channel (http://www.historychannel.com/broadband/home/). Perhaps the most beneficial aspect of filming student performances is that students (who can be their own worst critics) gain a new perspective on their appearance, enunciation, and nonverbal communication. The great advantage of using film to record student performance is that the subject under study is endlessly fascinating to students themselves.

FILM AS AN AESTHETIC EXPERIENCE

Although there are many possibilities for creating aesthetic experiences in school, I have found one activity to be particularly energizing and worthwhile—having students put images and sound to an original poem or short story.

A few years ago, I worked with a group of remedial students in a high school reading class. After these students wrote poems, they chose images and music to accompany their words. These pieces were assembled in PowerPoint presentations, with each slide displaying images and a line of poetry. Students recited poems using a microphone as they played their preselected music, and clicked through their slides. The writing resulting from those PowerPoint poems was uniformly high and represented quantum leaps in quality for most students (Baines, 2001).

Lately, I have transferred the basic idea—finding images and music to accompany words—from PowerPoint to film.

Lesson Idea

Begin with a student's original poem, preferably one that he or she actually likes and the teacher and peers consider meritorious. Have the class form cooperative groups of two or three. Peer-edit papers using the CSI (color, sound, images) method. Using the CSI editing process, students read a poem and respond by writing the following:

1. The poem's dominant colors,

2. Sounds and songs that come to mind, and

3. Images, places, or artworks that are elicited by the poem.

Peers should be as specific as possible in their comments. The idea is to get poets to begin thinking in multisensory terms about bringing their poems to life. What usually happens at this stage is that poets begin to make a few subtle revisions, substituting more precise and vibrant words where their descriptions may have been generic or clichéd.

Once editing is finished, poets use a storyboard for each line of the poem. A storyboard is simple enough to concoct—it is a series of boxes on a sheet of paper, usually four boxes per page. Every box has the following captions underneath: location, characters, time of day, and camera angle. The storyboard becomes an outline for the eventual film and, like all outlines, the final product may adhere to or digress from it.

Decide what elements should be present in films and communicate requirements clearly in an assessment rubric. Some criteria I have used in the past include a few shots of the poet, introductory and ending credits, clearly articulated language, symbolic imagery, and appropriate music.

Finally, students shoot their films. A digital camera is preferable because editing is easier with digitally shot film. However, a digital camera is not necessary—any camera will do. Assign the project on a Thursday or Friday and have completed films due the following Tuesday or Wednesday so that students have time to shoot and edit their work over a weekend. An example of a recent poetic film project (with stills extracted from the video) follows:

My soul is green
Green is my essence,
Born Libra of the air, craving balance,
I seek the ground.

Humus, loam, sand, clay, rock—
I burst forth with the slightest sustenance
Out of decay, torpid winter or torrid blaze
I wake.

I am warm, nearing yellow,
Yet cool, clean shade.
I am vivid sapling, emerging bud, timid sprout,
Poised on the seed of hope

New and naïve.

I am sea-green swirling, deep ancient myths
rising to the surface—

Glaucous veiled emeralds of truth

Old and sage.

I am dependent vine, seeking support.

I am ethereal fern, waving on the wind.

I am reliable succulent, carrying my
own water in my wings.

Lush, leafy, mossy verdure

The inaudible buzz of life

I germinate always

And nurtured

Flourish
Green.

Printed with permission from Karen Schoenberger.

CONCLUSION

Although moving images have become ubiquitous in the developed world, film is used sparingly as an instructional tool in K–12 schools. If film is used at all, it is often used poorly—to show a movie after the reading of a novel—or just to kill time.

Film is a teaching tool of unlimited variety and immense power. The modest exercises suggested here offer only an inkling of the rich possibilities for using film effectively in the classroom.

REFERENCES

Admussen, R. (1978). Novel into film: An experimental course. *Literature/Film Quarterly, 6*(1), 66–72.

Anderson, D. (1992). Using feature films as tools for analysis in a psychology and law course. *Teaching of Psychology, 19*(3), 155–158.

Anthon, C. (1899). *Manual of Greek literature from the earliest authentic periods to the close of the Byzantine era.* Ann Arbor, MI: University of Michigan.

Beckman, C., Austin, R., & Thompson, D. (2004). Exploring proportional reasoning through movies and literature. *Mathematics Teaching in the Middle School, 9*(5), 256–262.

Baines, L. (1995, February). Scripting screenplays: An idea for integrating reading, writing, and media literacy. *English Journal,* 86–91.

Baines, L. (1997, February). Dispensing with intellect. *Journal of Adolescent and Adult Literacy,* 385–386.

Baines, L. A. (2001, September). Out of the box. *Voices From the Middle,* 12–20.

Boutwell, W. (1952, March). What can we do about movies, radio, television? *English Journal,* 131–136.

Cennamo, K. (1993). Learning from video. Factors influencing learners' preconceptions and invested mental effort. *Educational Technology Research and Development, 41*(3), 33–45.

Center for American History. (2005). *"To whom was this sacrifice useful?" The Texas Revolution and the narrative of José Enrique de la Peña: An online exhibit.* Retrieved December 4, 2005, from http://www.cah.utexas.edu/exhibits/Pena/english/exhibit1.html

Charters, W. (1933). *Motion pictures and youth: A summary.* New York: Macmillan.

Costanzo, W. (1985). *Double exposure: Composing through writing and film.* Upper Montclair, NJ: Boynton/Cook.

Costanzo, W. (1992). *Reading the movies.* Urbana, IL: National Council of Teachers of English Press.

Costanzo, W. (2004). *Great films and how to teach them.* Urbana, IL: National Council of Teachers of English Press.

Gardner, P. (1991, October). Narrative crossings: Film adaptations in the literature class. *Teaching English in the Two-Year College,* 217–224.

Golden, J. (2006). *Reading in the reel world: Teaching documentaries and other nonfiction texts.* Urbana, IL: NCTE.

Higgins, J. (1991, Fall). Video pedagogy as political activity. *Journal of Film and Video, 18*–29.

Karl, H. (1981). What it means to be media competent. In C. Cooper (Ed.), *The nature and measurement of competency in English* (pp. 139–163). Urbana, IL: National Council of Teachers of English.

Kerber, C., Clemens, D., & Medina, W. (2004). Seeing is believing. *Journal of Nursing Education, 43*(10), 479.

Kraft, R. (1987). The influence of camera angle on comprehension and retention of pictorial events. *Memory & Cognition, 15,* 291–307.

Krendl, K. (1986). Media influence on learning. *Educational Communications Technology Journal, 34,* 223–234.

Larsson, D. (2001). *Survey: Use of film in Minnesota high schools Results.* Retrieved October 10, 2005, from http://english2.mnsu.edu/larsson/SCS/MNSurvey.html

Loewen, J. (1991, January). Teaching race relations from feature films. *Teaching Sociology,* 82–86.

Maynard, R. (1971). *The celluloid curriculum: How to use movies in the classroom.* Rochelle Park, NJ: Hayden.

McDonald, B. (1983). *Basic language skills through films.* Littleton, CO: Libraries Unlimited.

McNulty, E. (2005, October 28). Visual Parables Workshop. Collingwood Presbyterian Church, Toledo, Ohio.

Miller, H. (1979). *Films in the classroom: A practical guide.* Metuchen, NJ: Scarecrow.

Neal, R. (1913, December). Making the devil useful. *English Journal,* 658–660.

Remender, P. (1992). Using feature films to encourage critical thinking. *Southern Social Studies Journal, 17*(2), 33–44.

Resch, K., & Schicker, V. (1992). *Using film in the high school curriculum.* Jefferson, NC: McFarland.

Rosoff, M. (2004). *How I live now.* New York: Wendy Lamb Books.

Selby, S. (1978). *The study of film as an art form in American secondary schools.* New York: Arno Press.

Shiring, J. (1990, October). Free reading and film. *English Journal,* 37–40.

Squires, N. (1990). A Freireian-inspired video curriculum for at-risk high school students. *English Journal, 79*(2), 49–56.

Vetrie, M. (2004). Using film to increase literacy skills. *English Journal, 93*(3), 39–45.

Films Cited

Daly, J., & Gibson, D. (Producers), & Cameron, J. (Director). (1984). *The terminator* [Motion picture]. Los Angeles, CA: Hemdale.

Dayton, L. (Producer) & Tokar, N. (Director). (1974). *Where the red fern grows* [Motion picture]. Los Angeles, CA: Doty-Dayton.

Hallowell, T. (Producer), & Hancock, J. (Director). (2004). *The Alamo* [Motion picture]. Los Angeles, CA: Buena Vista.

Huston, J. (Producer & Director). (1956). *Moby Dick* [Motion picture]. Burbank, CA: Warner Brothers.

Jaffe, S. (Executive Producer), & Zucker, J. (Director). (1990). *Ghost* [Motion picture]. Los Angeles, CA: Paramount.

Lazar, A. (Producer), & Junger, G. (Director). (1999). *10 things I hate about you* [Motion picture]. Los Angeles, CA: Buena Vista.

Luhrmann, B. (Producer & Director). (1996). *Romeo + Juliet* [Motion picture]. Los Angeles, CA: 20th-Century Fox.

Milchan, A., & Reuther, S. (Producers), & Marshall, G. (Director). (1990). *Pretty woman* [Motion picture]. Los Angeles: Touchstone.

Ruddy, A. (Producer), & Coppola, F. (Director). (1972). *The godfather* [Motion picture]. Los Angeles, CA: Paramount.

Wayne, J. (Producer & Director). (1960). *The Alamo* [Motion picture]. Burbank, CA: United Artists.

9

"It Was Always the Pictures . . . "

Creating Visual Literacy Supports for Students With Disabilities

Paula Kluth

In what ways do visual literacy approaches make it possible for students with disabilities to demonstrate what they know? Read how Kluth uses interactive strategies to ensure access to the general education curriculum.

Many students appreciate the opportunity to learn in a classroom where visual supports are provided. This is certainly true for many students with disabilities who struggle with traditional presentations of content like lecture and whole-class discussion. Many learners with disabilities, including those with autism, some learning disabilities, and some cognitive disabilities learn best when they have an image of what they are learning. In a study by Hibbing and Rankin-Erickson (2003), one struggling reader said, "If you look at a picture, it puts more ideas in your head." And Donna Williams (1992), a woman with autism, observed, "Though I could read a story without difficulty, it was always the pictures from which I understood the content" (p. 25). She has also shared that visuals have always helped to guide her learning in expository texts. She claims that she "took to" the study of psychology in part because it was connected to her personal experiences (she had been evaluated by a lot of psychologists and psychiatrists), but also because her course materials were filled with pictures:

> A lot of psychology had to do with finding out how things worked. The subject of the mind was, for me, like the study of an object that worked according to a system . . .
>
> The textbook had a lot of pictures and diagrams, which made the rest of the text easy to follow. (p. 119)

STUDENTS WITH DISABILITIES AND VISUAL SUPPORTS

One reason for providing visual supports is that many learners labeled with disabilities are clearly visual learners and are thus best able to understand and remember content when they can see it graphically represented in some way. Students who are deaf and hard of hearing, for instance, will appreciate seeing information in addition to "hearing" about it via sign language, an interpreter, lip reading, or other technology. Students with learning disabilities who often have difficulty learning through one or more "channels" report that they can be more successful when the teacher uses visual strategies and methods in addition to or in lieu of a traditional lecture or discussion format. And some with autism report that pictures are the very way in which they understand and derive meaning from the world: "Words are like a second language to me. I translate both spoken and written words into full-color movies, complete with sound, which run like a VCR tape in my head. When somebody speaks to me, his words are instantly translated into pictures" (Grandin, 1995, p. 1).

Visual and spatial learners like the individuals described in the preceding paragraph often think visually and learn best from things that can be seen, including handouts, movies, diagrams, charts, and graphic organizers, illustrated books, learning-related objects (e.g., globe, manipulatives), PowerPoint presentations or overhead transparencies, pictures, and checklists. Each of these supports can be offered across subject areas, can be used to boost literacy learning, and can be generated by teachers or by students themselves.

Further, providing visual supports in the classroom is good insurance that a wider range of learners will be reached. In inclusive classrooms, the teacher is often concerned about using a variety of teaching tools and strategies so that he or she can meet the needs of students with disabilities, but this same teacher often finds that using several different strategies, techniques, methods, and tools increases and enhances the learning of all students in the classroom, not just those with identified needs.

Helpful Strategies: Literacy Learning Through Visual Information

Five visual supports helpful for teaching and supporting literacy development are described here: graphic organizers, picture books, fascination-focused materials, graphic notes, and story kits. Some of these are "old favorites" (e.g., graphic organizers) and are being shared here for the purpose of illustrating how these techniques can be adapted for students with disabilities. Others are new, developed specifically for students with disabilities but often equally as effective for students without disability labels (e.g., story kits).

These ideas may be effective for working with *some* students with disabilities and each may be used as a take-off point for designing literacy lessons that are appropriate, appealing, and challenging for learners with unique learning characteristics. Specific examples of how each can profit students with learning, sensory, or physical differences are shared.

Graphic Organizers

Graphic organizers, also known as concept maps or diagrams, advance or cognitive organizers, flow charts, or story maps are visual displays of knowledge that structure information by arranging important aspects of an idea, term, or topic into a pattern and by showing relationships between related concepts (Bromley, 1996; Bromley, Devitas, & Modlo, 1999). They are effective teaching tools in that they help students to represent abstract ideas in more concrete ways, to store and recall information, to demonstrate relationships among facts and concepts, and to organize ideas (Billmeyer & Barton, 1998; Bromley, Devitas, & Modlo, 1999). Examples of graphic organizers include Venn diagrams, cause and effect frameworks, semantic webs, series-of-events chains, network trees, cycle maps, and flow charts.

Teachers use graphic organizers in a variety of ways, often including them as a supplement for their lectures or whole-class discussions, especially when they are supporting students with and without disabilities in inclusive classrooms. For instance, when the class is studying a novel, the teacher might provide students with a pictorial timeline of the events in the story. Or he might use a Venn diagram to show learners how to compare and contrast two time periods in history. Such applications of graphic organizers can help all students better understand the content, connect the new learning to concepts they already understand, and make abstract concepts more concrete. Graphic organizers may be especially useful in supporting the literacy development of students with disabilities, however, as these visual tools reduce the cognitive demands on the learner. In other words, the student does not need to "process as much semantic information to understand the information" (Ellis, 2004).

Teachers can use graphic organizers in a variety of ways. They can use them before a lesson to activate or assess prior knowledge, teach or review vocabulary, and pre-teach concepts and ideas related to the text. Organizers can also be used during a lesson to help students follow the text and remain focused on the task. Finally, these tools can be used after a lesson to review the new learning and to reinforce the content.

And using graphic organizers in the inclusive classroom can profit all learners, not just those struggling with reading and writing. Researchers have found that students with and without disabilities can profit from the use of graphic organizers (Boyle & Weishaar, 1997; Darch et al., 1986; Gardill & Jitendra, 1999). Specifically, many studies have suggested that the use of graphic organizers can help learners improve both comprehension (Boyle & Weishaar, 1997; Idol & Croll, 1987) and vocabulary knowledge (Moore & Readence, 1984).

These tools can also help learners understand how texts are structured. While skilled readers may not need help in comprehending how a passage, chapter, or book has been arranged, struggling readers are likely to need such support. The National Reading Panel (2000) reported, in fact, that learners were better able to answer questions and recall what they read when they received instruction not only in content, but also in story organization.

When using graphic organizers in the inclusive classroom, educators may want to consider the following adaptations, ideas, and implementation tips:

- If some students in the classroom are emerging readers, then icons, images, or pictures should be paired with words whenever possible. The teacher should be sure, however, to teach the meaning of the icons, images, or pictures as students may be even more confused when unclear or unfamiliar graphics are used to make text easier to comprehend (see Figure 9.1).

Figure 9.1

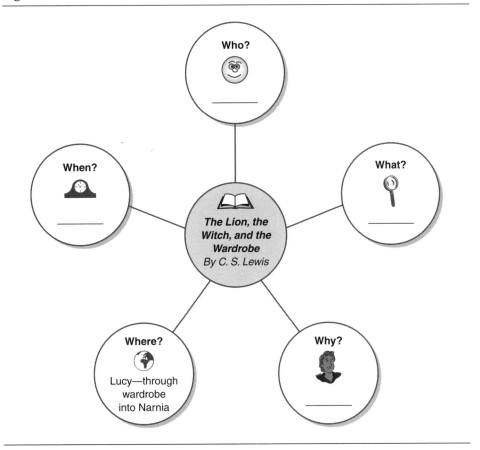

- Many students will need practice and guidance as they learn to use organizers. Students should have many opportunities to see the teacher develop and use a range of different graphic organizers before they are asked to use them as learning tools. Since it is sometimes hard for a teacher to talk and illustrate her discussion at the same time, many teachers rely on another adult to co-teach this type of lesson with them. A general educator might work with a special educator, paraprofessional, speech and language therapist, or even another student to "show and tell" about graphic organizers.

- Students with more significant disabilities may not be able to construct or fill in the components of a graphic organizer. For this type of learner, alternative materials can be used that would allow the student to create or manipulate a diagram without being able to write or draw. For instance, a student can be given cards or magnetic pieces to assemble for a timeline. Or this same learner may be able to use a program such as Kidspiration® (software that helps students

Figure 9.2

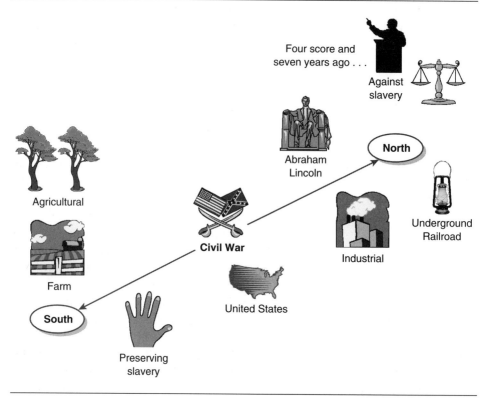

SOURCE: Diagram created in Kidspiration® by Inspiration Software®, Inc.

build graphic organizers by combining pictures, text, and spoken words) to create a visual representation of ideas (http://www .inspiration.com/productinfo/kidspiration/index.cfm). See Figure 9.2 for an organizer constructed using this technology.

- In addition to teaching from graphic organizers, students should be given opportunities to construct their own organizers. Teaching students how to create these tools will help them learn how to approach complex text on their own. Students should be given plenty of time and ample opportunity to learn how to create organizers before they are asked to attempt this with partners or on their own.
- Graphic organizers can be used to teach more than reading. When students are taught to read and develop graphic organizers, they can also learn critical thinking, organization, and communication skills. What are the needs of individual students in the classroom? Can individual goals (e.g., individual education plan objectives) be taught through the use of graphic organizers? If a student with a

disability is working on note taking skills, for instance, he or she might be taught how to do so using a graphic organizer such as a semantic web. Or a learner might be taught how to follow along with a whole-class discussion by tracking topics on a flow chart or series-of-events map.

Picture Books

Picture books combine words and pictures to tell a story. Typically, in these texts, the pictures don't just supplement the text; they are as important or central as the text. An example of this would be *Pink and Say* (Polacco, 1994), a gorgeous and powerful book based on a true story of two young men, one black and one white, during the U.S. Civil War. The text would certainly work well alone, but when it is paired with the rough and poignant illustrations of the two men helping each other survive and hiding out from fellow soldiers, the story becomes compelling and captivating.

Picture books are often used in the early elementary grades, but they can actually be quite effective for students in older grades, including middle and high school levels. Picture books can be used as primary texts to introduce and examine an issue or as supplementary texts for learners needing extra support. For instance, a middle school science teacher used *A River Ran Wild: An Environmental History* (Cherry, 1992), a story about the Nashua River of New Hampshire, to teach all learners in the class about conservation and pollution. The text includes not only a story of the river itself but also contrasting maps of New England (in the 1500s and in the 1900s) and an author's note detailing the work of a committee who organized to clean up the Nashua.

The teacher used the book to launch a project where students studied a river in their own town. They researched the river's ending and beginning, the rivers and brooks that feed it, the general condition of the water, and the ways in which their city polluted and protected the river. While all learners seemed to benefit and learn from the project, the visual learners in the classroom and, in particular, a handful of students with learning disabilities appeared to appreciate the teacher's approach and use of nontraditional materials. One student with reading difficulties was so intrigued by the project, in fact, that he offered to *make* picture books for other science units during the year so other students with learning problems would be able to learn sophisticated content from a source that was less complex than the textbook.

Of course, there are many print materials aside from picture books that include illustrations, drawings, photographs, and other visual supplements. Educators should also seek out these texts to use in their teaching, given that so many learners note that their comprehension is boosted when they have the benefit of visual information.

When using picture books or other illustrated texts in the inclusive classroom, educators may want to consider the following adaptations, ideas, and implementation tips:

- Does the classroom library offer a range of choices for all learning styles and levels? Does it offer different versions of the same text (e.g., traditional copy, illustrated version, and comic book of *Romeo and Juliet*) so all students can access challenging content and sophisticated literature?
- Will classroom literature and other written materials need to be adapted for use by some students? Teachers can adapt picture books by enlarging text, highlighting key words or passages, summarizing or simplifying the language throughout, or adding a graphic organizer to help the student track characters or plot. Students with certain learning difficulties may also profit from use of Kurzweil text-to-speech software (http://www.kurzweiledu.com/default .aspx), which scans text and allows students to "read" it by viewing the book on screen and listening (and following along) as it is read.
- Examine lesson plans across content areas. Is it possible to use picture books as a teaching tool in some of these plans? In upper grades, the picture book can be used as a supplement for class discussions and as a primary text for those students who are struggling readers.
- Could students create their own picture books as a way to boost their interest and comprehension? Where in the curriculum might this be appropriate? For some students, the creation of a picture book can serve as an assessment of learning. After reading a piece of text or listening to a lecture, students can be asked to reconstruct the material in the form of a book that can be shared with peers.
- Do a review of classroom texts (picture books, textbooks, etc.). Do they, in general, have a range of graphic supports (e.g., charts, photographs, illustrations) that might appeal to different learners in the classroom? Does the textbook series offer ancillary materials that could help visual learners (e.g., posters, transparencies, software)?
- Not all learners will be able to make sense of pictures as easily as others. Teachers must be aware that some learners will need prompting to notice and gather information from the graphics in text. In the useful book *Supporting Struggling Readers and Writers,* the authors suggest that educators wanting to model how students can learn from visuals use a collaborative think-aloud strategy. Teachers can select an image from the text they are teaching, share their thoughts about what they see and how they react to what they see. Following this exercise, the educator can ask students to "turn and talk" to a partner about their impressions of the image so they can get even more feedback about how different learners understand and use visuals.

Fascination-Focused Materials

Another way to engage students and possibly elevate their literacy skills is to create fascination-focused materials. Fascination-focused materials can be used with any student but are often most effective for those learners with intense and sometimes interfering interests such as students with autism and Asperger's syndrome. Many individuals with autism have a deep interest in a single topic or in a variety of specific topics. Some interests are commonly seen across individuals with autism (e.g., trains, horses, light switches), while others seem more unique to an individual person. For instance, Sean Barron, a man with autism, once had a deep interest in the number 24. At another point in his life, he became fascinated by dead-end streets (Barron & Barron, 1992).

Any similar specific student interests might be used as part of the curriculum. Too often, teachers of students with these "obsessions" try to discourage the student from spending time on or with their special possessions or interests. However, this approach often does little to diminish the student's appetite for his area of passion. Further, key learning opportunities may be lost. For example, a student who loves trains might be asked to write a story about riding on a caboose, to research different railroads on the Internet, or to do an independent project on ground transportation in America. These interests can also be used to develop materials that will help students with literacy learning. For instance, Trey, a student with autism, had a difficult time engaging in typical classroom activities; he seemed disinterested in textbooks, workbooks, work sheets, and art supplies. Trey's teacher tried to interest him in classroom activities by buying him some horse magazines. She hoped that he might be able to look at the magazines during breaks or after he finished class work. When she got the magazines and showed them to Trey, however, the plan crumbled. Not only did this strategy fail to engage Trey, but it made the situation worse. Trey was more distracted than ever. He couldn't concentrate on class work when the horse magazines were in the room. He would rummage through his desk to find them the moment he came into the classroom and would pore over them during daily lessons.

Trey's teacher solved the problem by creating classroom books using the magazine pictures. She made a social studies book from horse pictures (the topic was transportation, so she cut out pictures of horses pulling carts and people riding on horses). She also made a reading book by taking vocabulary from class lessons and creating a short story about horses. Trey was very interested in the adapted materials; he was able to stay with the class during lessons and could flip through his books if he needed to fidget. He was also able to learn new standards-based content by reading and rereading the horse books with teachers and classmates.

In another instance, Joe, a student with Down syndrome, was introduced to new vocabulary words when his teachers created a Harry Potter dictionary for him. Joe struggled to learn new vocabulary words and often retreated from lessons by paging through Harry Potter picture books. In response to his interest, his teachers developed a learning tool that would both push Joe to learn new words and honor his main expertise and interest area. New concepts and words were connected to words and concepts he had already mastered from watching Harry Potter movies and enjoying the books. For instance, the entry for "aloft," a vocabulary word, included a drawing of Harry Potter playing quidditch, flying through the air on his stick. The entry for "terrified" shows Harry encountering ghouls in the hallways of his wizard school. Joe is drawn to such materials due to his passion for Harry Potter, and, therefore, gets his assigned work completed.

When using fascination-focused materials in the inclusive classroom, educators may want to consider the following adaptations, ideas, and implementation tips:

- Knowing student interests can help teachers develop curriculum, instruction, and even behavior support strategies. Therefore, every teacher should know the interests and areas of expertise of the students in the classroom. How can this information be acquired if teachers don't already have it?
- Think of the learners in the classroom. Do any of them need curricular adaptations? Do any of them have intense interests? If so, would fascination-focused literature, dictionaries, word walls, or other materials enhance their literacy learning?
- Colleagues may be able to help in the creation and use of fascination books. If these tools are appropriate for certain learners, several different professionals or support staff might assist in developing the books. Who might help in creating these supports for learners in the classroom? Would speech therapists, librarians, teaching assistants, or reading specialists be able to help?
- Are there ways to use fascination books for all students in the classroom? Could all students in the classroom benefit from creating their own fascination-focused materials? In one classroom, the teacher allowed all students to review challenging vocabulary words (e.g., "reclusive," "solitude," "trite") by developing fascination-focused alphabet books on the topic of their choosing. One student drew intricate pictures of fantasy characters (e.g., unicorns), another used images of modern art, while another student with cognitive disabilities used digital photos of her classmates (and got to socialize and connect with each one in the process).

Graphic Notes

Drawing or graphic note taking is another strategy for boosting the literacy learning of students with disabilities. Modeling, teaching, and encouraging this strategy is a way to demonstrate that there are many different ways to represent information while giving struggling readers a way to share their understanding of a text, tell a story, or organize information.

An example of how graphic notes can be used to enhance comprehension comes from a high school biology teacher. This teacher, Ms. Kinch, supported the literacy development of her student, Shu-li, a student with cognitive disabilities, by asking the young woman to announce the "vocabulary word of the day" to all students in the class. While Shu-li and a peer partner read the word and definition, different students took turns trying to illustrate the word on chart paper. This artistic and collaborative exercise often drew laughter from the class as students attempted to draw terms such as "photosynthesis" and "meiosis." This exercise, while designed primarily to support Shu-li, enhanced the vocabulary of all learners and was, therefore, eventually used in all of the teacher's science classes. As Shu-li became more acquainted with the process of visually representing concepts, she gained confidence in taking class notes. While she had always been passive during teacher lectures, she eventually began sketching as the teacher talked and eventually had notebooks filled with representations of all of the class discussions.

Drawings, like the ones done by the biology students, can show teachers how students understand material. They can provide teachers with critical information on what students do or do not understand. For instance, Hibbing and Rankin-Erickson (2003) reported the story of a student who read a popular-fiction account of children during the Holocaust. The young man drew a detailed drawing of Hitler, but the image did not relate to the day's reading at all. The drawing, therefore, became the launching point for a conversation that clarified some areas of confusion for the learner and helped him to better comprehend the remainder of the text. When working with students with some disabilities, the opposite may also be true, so teachers must proceed with caution, as many of the drawings of students with fine-motor difficulties may actually contain relevant information but be hard to decipher by anyone but the student.

For instance, Glenn, a student with autism, used visual notes to track his understanding of the texts he chose for independent reading. When he read *The Devlin Affair* (Marlowe, 1987), a mystery about a private eye who is assigned to take a suitcase to Mexico City, Glenn tracked his reading by drawing a map and illustrating the events as they unfolded (see Figure 9.3). In his drawing, Glenn included arrows to mark Dev's travels, several of the settings of the book, and the FBI building. He also drew the suitcase with the false bottom (in the top left corner); this is a detail that might be missed by those who can't "read" Glenn's drawing easily. On a separate sheet of paper Glenn listed the names of the main characters and a story summary. His sketch and related text then became a tool that, though simple, was remarkably effective in guiding him through the reading. Not only that, it could also be referenced again as he read later chapters, answered questions about the story, and completed related classroom projects.

Students can be encouraged and taught to use visual notes in a variety of ways. One teacher simply told her students to take notes as they always had but to add "pictures, diagrams, doodles, patterns, or charts" in the margins or

Figure 9.3

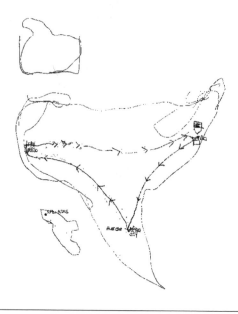

in the actual body of the notes to emphasize points, elaborate on an idea, or to make the content memorable. Another teacher showed a student with physical disabilities and limited mobility how to take visual notes using the computer. After reading *To Kill a Mockingbird* (Lee, 1960), the student searched the Web for images of law, slavery, schools, reading, injustice, spooky houses, family, and racism. He then assembled these images and some simple text into a PowerPoint presentation that he shared with classmates and used to answer comprehension questions posed by his teachers (see Figure 9.4).

Figure 9.4

To Kill a Mockingbird
Author Harper Lee
Aria and Amie

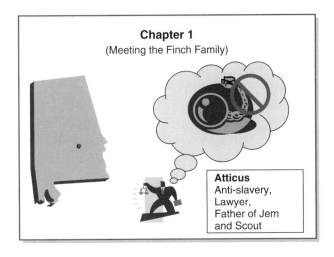

Another strategy that teachers can use to teach graphic note taking is mind mapping (Margulies, 2002). Mind mapping is a method of recording abstract information in a concrete way; the note taker simply draws small icons or pictures to represent what he or she hears or sees or otherwise learns. This strategy might be especially helpful for students with disabilities who struggle to represent ideas quickly or succinctly or to make sense of those ideas when referring to them at a later time. To teach mind mapping to students, the teacher should first provide them with larger sheets of paper than usual and ask them to follow along as the strategy is modeled. Teachers can demonstrate by sketching on the chalkboard or easel during a lecture or discussion and asking students to draw along with her at their desks or to take turns "illustrating" the classroom conversation. As key ideas are mentioned, students write them on lines that branch from the central image. Entire sentences are not necessary. The size of the words, the associated images, and the shapes that surround the words can be used for emphasis.

As students mimic the work of the teacher, they should be encouraged to develop their own symbols and codes. Students should be encouraged to think about all of the common symbols they know and could use in their drawings (e.g., a heart for love or romance, a puzzle piece for confusion or for something unresolved) in their drawings. They can also be prompted to generate original symbols for ideas or concepts they don't know how to represent.

Mind mapping can be used to share the daily schedule, encourage brainstorming, or record the learning in a lesson. It is especially useful for students with processing difficulties or fine-motor problems, as these students may be at a loss when asked to represent concepts in ways that others can easily understand. Teaching all students easy-to-use symbols is one way to avoid the inevitable "I can't draw!" protest.

For a literacy lesson, mind mapping can be used as a way to take notes and make predictions before a reading or a text, to record impressions during a reading of a text, or to assess what the learner knows. In one classroom, students developed a set of symbols for key characters and ideas when they studied *Of Mice and Men* (Steinbeck, 1937) in order to take notes more efficiently and share ideas with one another quickly. Students then shared their maps when they engaged in small-group discussions of each chapter. One student with physical disabilities, who did not have reliable use of his hands, worked on a collaborative drawing with a peer. He contributed by suggesting ideas for the map and by affixing stickers representing key ideas to appropriate parts of the drawing (see Figure 9.5).

Lastly, students could also be taught story mapping (Boulineau, Fore, Hagan-Burke, & Burke, 2004; Sorrell, 1990) as a visual note-taking tool. This structure is a more linear way to capture information; students can be taught

Figure 9.5

to map out events in an artistic and symbolic way by drawing a path or trail and inserting images as they move through the story. Or they can map by taking visual notes in chronological order in a notebook or in consecutive boxes on a page. For example, a fifth-grade teacher had her students map out *The Summer of the Swans* (Byars, 1970) using an exercise she

Figure 9.6

calls four-corner comprehension; this simply involves having small groups of students read sections of text (in this case, chapters) and then pause to draw or map what they read at the end of each section (see Figure 9.6).

When using visual notes in the inclusive classroom, educators may want to consider the following adaptations, ideas, and implementation tips:

- Could all students be taught a visual note taking strategy as a way to increase their interest in the classroom activities and enhance their understanding of the content? Are there students who would need adaptations to take notes in this way? Students with fine-motor challenges might use stickers, rubber stamps, or the computer to create their notes. PowerPoint will allow students to insert pictures and words easily. And Microsoft Word will allow students to insert symbols and clip art as well.
- Are there specific note-taking strategies (e.g., mind mapping) some or all learners should be taught to give them new tools for organizing and retaining information?
- Many students including active and artistic learners like doodling and drawing, in general. As an experiment, a teacher might allow

students to illustrate their daily work as a way of enhancing attention and understanding. Students can then be asked to report on how the strategy helped or impacted their learning. Or an assessment related to the graphic notes can be designed to measure student growth and understanding.

- Not all students will know how to draw for meaning. Are there students in the classroom who would need instruction in drawing or visual note taking? For these students, it can help to do some modeling, to encourage practice, to share and display examples, and to specifically teach how different simple icons can represent different ideas or concepts (e.g., a star could represent evening, a "bright" idea, or something important to remember; a road can represent a journey, growth, a trip, or a connection between two things or ideas).

Story Kits

Finally, for students with more significant disabilities or for those who are blind or have limited vision, a teacher might consider the use of story kits as a way to improve literacy learning. Story kits can help a reader generate ideas, retain information, and further their understanding of a particular idea or concept.

A story kit is simply a bag or box of items related to a theme, unit, or particular story. A story kit for *Island of the Blue Dolphins* (Dell, 1960), for instance, contained a stuffed dog, a small toy canoe, a rock, some sand or water in a vial, a small box of "jewels," and a dolphin figurine. The kit can be used to introduce the story, to review it and/or to interest and support students as they enjoy and discuss the story, and to give them cues as they engage in other activities related to the book (e.g., writing a book report). Teachers using this type of support should also, of course, include a copy of the book adapted for that particular learner (Downing, 2005). Some students may profit from a tactile book with teacher-added textures or objects while others may need large-print versions of the text.

Of course, these kits don't need to be limited to use with particular stories or books. Kits can be assembled to teach general ideas or concepts (e.g., setting), types of literature/writing (e.g., autobiography), and even individual authors (e.g., Shakespeare). One first-grade teacher, for instance, asked all of her students to participate in creating kits that could be used by all students in the classroom, especially one child with Down syndrome who needed help understanding abstract concepts. One kit that the class spent weeks assembling and modifying was the one representing fairy tales, a theme they explored across different areas of the curriculum. The kit contained a few finger puppets (a princess, a frog, three bears, a wolf, and a grandma), a "magic" wand, a plastic beanstalk, and a red cape.

When using story kits in the inclusive classroom, educators may want to consider the following adaptations, ideas, and implementation tips:

- Story kits can be used for more than one purpose; for what specific purpose might story kits be used across grade levels and content areas (e.g., to help students recall story details, to give students ideas for creative writing related to the story, to "illustrate" a retelling of a story or of a set of facts)?
- When working with students with significant disabilities, especially one with physical or communication difficulties, it will be important to use the story kit in the classroom (not just give it to the student to use). For instance, in a second-grade classroom, when students read *Duck for President,* the teacher (or a student) held up various objects from the kit during every reading of the text. For example, every time there was a vote in the story, the teacher or students held up a little ballot box. And when students participated in the discussion afterward, they were encouraged to use the objects too. After seeing eight classmates use the objects to react to the story, Stacie, a child with significant physical and communication differences, was able to use the objects to do the same.
- Students can create personal or classroom story kits for different texts. What guidelines should be given for the creation of these kits and how can they be used to give different support to different learners? In other words, how might story kits be used as a tool for differentiating instruction and how can students with and without disabilities profit from the use of story kits?
- Can kits be created for books or selections that are not fiction? What would a "story kit" for a chapter in a high school science textbook look like? How would the assembly of such kits help literacy learning?

CONCLUSIONS

In years past, many students with disabilities were excluded not only from general education classrooms but also from meaningful literacy instruction. Today, these same learners are gaining increasing access to inclusive, motivating, and appropriately challenging literacy experiences. This is happening, in part, because teachers are changing and expanding the strategies and methods used in daily lessons.

Using more visual supports is just one way that effective teachers are meeting the needs of a wider range of learners. All the strategies in this chapter can certainly be used for students with and without disabilities in inclusive classrooms, but they may have the most impact on those learners who cannot learn effectively in classrooms using traditional tools and strategies. With the increased use of computers and the Internet, a wider than ever selection of print materials, and the growing attention to differentiation and using diverse materials in the classroom, students with a host of learning needs can be included in the literate community in ways they have never been included before. By expanding the strategies used in the classroom and, specifically, by expanding the use of visual supports in literacy instruction, teachers are sure to reach a wider range of learners and to give every student opportunities to hone their skills as listeners, speakers, writers, and readers.

REFERENCES

Alvermann, D. E., & Boothby, P. R. (1986). Children's transfer of graphic organizer instruction. *Reading Psychology, 7*(2), 87–100.

Barron, J., & Barron, S. (1992). *There's a boy in here.* New York: Simon & Schuster.

Billmeyer, R., & Barton, M. (1998). *Teaching reading in the content areas: If not me, then who?* Aurora, CO: Mid-Continent Regional Educational Laboratory.

Boulineau , T., Fore, C., Hagan-Burke, S., & Burke, M. (2004). Use of story-mapping to increase the story-grammar text comprehension of elementary students with learning disabilities. *Learning Disability Quarterly, 27,* 105–121.

Boyle, J. R., & Weishaar, M. (1997). The effects of expert-generated versus student-generated cognitive organizers on the reading comprehension of students with learning disabilities. *Learning Disabilities Research & Practice, 12*(4), 228–235.

Bromley, K. D. (1996). *Webbing with literature: Creating story maps with children's books* (2nd ed.). Needham Heights, MA: Allyn & Bacon.

Bromley, K., Irwin Devitis, L., & Modlo, M. (1999). *50 graphic organizers for reading, writing & more: Reproducible templates, student samples, and easy strategies to support every learner.* New York: Scholastic Professional Books.

Byars, B. (1970). *The summer of the swans.* New York: Puffin.

Cherry, L. (1992). *A river ran wild: An environmental history.* New York: Gulliver Green.

Cronin, D. (2004). *Duck for president.* New York: Simon & Schuster.

Dell, S. (1960). *Island of the blue dolphins.* Yearling.

Downing, J. (2005). *Teaching literacy to students with significant disabilities.* Thousand Oaks, CA: Corwin Press.

Gardill, M. C., & Jitendra, A. K. (1999). Advanced story map instruction: Effects on the reading comprehension of students with learning disabilities. *The Journal of Special Education, 33*(1), 2–17.

Grandin, T. (1995). *Thinking in pictures.* New York: Vintage Books.

Griffon, C., Malone, L., & Kameenui, E. (2001). Effects of graphic organizer instruction on fifth-grade students. *The Journal of Educational Research, 89*(2), 98–107.

Hibbing, A., & Rankin-Erickson, J. L. (2003). "A picture is worth a thousand words": Using visual images to improve comprehension for middle school struggling readers. *The Reading Teacher, 56,* 8.

Idol, L., & Croll, V. J. (1987). Story-mapping training as a means of improving reading comprehension. *Learning Disability Quarterly, 10*(3), 214–229.

Lee, H. (1960). *To kill a mockingbird.* London: Heinemann.

Margulies, N. (1990). *Mapping inner space.* Tucson, AZ: Zephyr Press.

Marlowe, D. (1987). *The Devlin affair.* Belmont, CA: Fearon.

Mayer, R. E., Bove, W., Bryman, A., Mars, R., & Tapangco, L. (1996). When less is more: Meaningful learning from visual and verbal summaries of science textbook lessons. *Journal of Educational Psychology, 88*(1), 64–73.

Merkley, D. M., & Jefferies, D. (2001). Guidelines for implementing a graphic organizer. *The Reading Teacher, 54*(4), 350–357.

Moore, D. W., & Readence, J. E. (1984). A quantitative and qualitative review of graphic organizer research. *Journal of Educational Research, 78*(1), 11–17. National Reading Panel.

Newby, R. F., Caldwell, J., & Recht, D. R. (1989). Improving the reading comprehension of children with dysphonetic and dyseidetic dyslexia using story grammar. *Journal of Learning Disabilities, 22(6),* 373–380.

Polacco, P. (1994). *Pink and Say.* New York: Philomel.

Sinatra, R. (1986). Visual literacy connections to thinking, reading and writing. Springfield, IL: Charles C Thomas.

Sinatra, R. C., Stahl-Gemake, J., & Berg, D. N. (1984). Improving reading comprehension of disabled readers through semantic mapping. *The Reading Teacher, 38*(1), 22–29.

Sorrell, A. L. (1990). Three reading comprehension strategies: TELLS, story mapping, and QARs. *Academic Therapy, 25,* 359–368.

Steinbeck, J. (1937). *Of mice and men.* New York: Covici-Friede.

Strickland, D. S., Ganske, K., & Monroe, J. (2002). *Supporting struggling readers and writers.* Portland, ME: Stenhouse.

Tarquin, P., & Walker, S. (1997). *Creating success in the classroom! Visual organizers and how to use them.* Englewood, CO: Teacher Ideas Press.

Vallecorsa, A. L., & deBettencourt, L. U. (1997). Using a mapping procedure to teach reading and writing skills to middle grade students with learning disabilities. *Education and Treatment of Children, 20,* 173–189.

Willerman, M., & Mac Harg, R. A. (1991). The concept map as an advance organizer. *Journal of Research in Science Teaching, 28*(8), 705–712.

Williams, D. (1992). *Nobody nowhere.* New York: Avon.

Index

CORWIN PRESS